BLESS HER HEART

To our parents:
Big Jim and Kathy
and
Dr. Al and Carol

BLESS HER HEART

Life as a Young Clergy Woman

Ashley-Anne Masters
&
Stacy Smith

CHALICE
PRESS
ST. LOUIS, MISSOURI

Bible quotations, unless otherwise noted, are from the *New Revised Standard Version Bible,* copyright 1989, Division of Christian Education of the National Council of the Churches of Christ in the United States of America. Used by permission. All rights reserved.

Cover image: Copyright© Chantal Parè
Cover and interior design: Scribe Inc.

www.ChalicePress.com

10 9 8 7 6 5 4 3 2 1   11 12 13 14 15 16 17

EPUB: 9780827202771   EPDF: 9780827202788

Library of Congress Cataloging-in-Publication Data
Masters, Ashley-Anne.
  Bless her heart : life as a young clergy woman / Ashley-Anne Masters and Stacy Smith.
     p. cm.
  ISBN 978-0-8272-0276-4
  1. Women clergy. I. Smith, Stacy. II. Title.
  BV676.M375 2011
  248.8'92–dc23   2011031371

Printed in United States of America

Contents

959

124197

Foreword

Every spring, as the Introduction to Preaching course starts at Columbia, I hold my breath: maybe *this* will be the year when my students will be able to utter the words "preacher" and "woman" in the same breath, without apology, defense, or well-intended overcompensation. Maybe *this* will be the year when a woman preacher is just no big deal—or at least, no bigger deal than a man preacher. Maybe all those fervent debates I hear in workshop about earrings (too distracting?) and heels (too high?) will have taken their place in the historical compost of former times, alongside the advice once given to men preachers at our seminary (I'm told) to wear dark socks.

I am waiting for the day when my students will see themselves—and their peers!—as preachers first, rather than *women* preachers and *men* preachers. Because that will be the day we can get onto the business of being *human* preachers, whom God created male and female, with all types of bodies and all ranges of voices and all manners of taste in music, dress, shoes, and tattoos. It will save a lot of time.

Ashley-Anne Masters and Stacy Smith have created something wonderful, here. They have taken a shortcut past the historical debates of past generations (*are women allowed to preach?*) and seminary classes (*do women really preach differently than men?*) and jumped right into the deep end of experience—*their* experience. Every generation has to do it, eventually. We have to swim in our own pool. And we will swim differently than the ones who went before us, because the pool is different, and so are the questions we ask and the strokes we use. Masters and Smith know this, and so they haven't wasted time with outmoded verbs like "explain" or "defend" or "apologize," when it comes to their own pool. They have jumped straight to "bless," a verb that is much deeper and harder to embody. What does it look like to be a preacher blessed to be a preacher, no matter who you are? What does it look like today, for young women? How can we do the coming-of-age work that every generation must take up, which is to reframe the questions and blessings of another context to fit our own?

I am thrilled that Masters and Smith took up the challenge to write this book. The voices they lift up, the wisdom they share, will surely empower other preachers, young and old, to reach for the deeper verbs.

Anna Carter Florence
Columbia Theological Seminary

Preface

In February of 2010, we met up in Memphis to finish the last few chapters of this book. When it came to dating, preaching, shoes, and Sabbath, we had plenty of information to work with. As colleagues, we met in 2008 and became friends through the sharing of our stories over coffee or a cocktail. Our experiences as young women, newly ordained in the Presbyterian Church (USA) and working in a large church with lots of women of different ages and backgrounds, gave us firsthand knowledge about living the life of a young female pastor. And then there were our other friends. One by one, as more colleagues got ordained and started working in ministry, we began to hear about the infuriating and inspiring things that were going on in their lives. We joined the Young Clergy Women Project and read *Fidelia's Sisters*, which gives us a space to discuss our issues, joys, and daily challenges. So when we brainstormed this book proposal, we were immediately drawn to our stories and the stories of women we know. We wanted to share them in a way that was honestly critical and spiritually uplifting.

In the midst of those last few days of writing, we started seeing Facebook updates from other young clergy women about an upcoming event: On TLC's "What Not to Wear," they were making over a twenty-six-year-old Episcopal priest named Emily Bloemker. This was to be a night of must-see-television for all the young clergy women throughout the land. We spent the afternoon writing at the coffee shop and then came home to see the simple, eloquent, and inspiring Emily step into the 360-degree mirror and shine a light on the realities of women in ministry.

She began saying that while she had been confident in her abilities and her personality, she had lacked confidence in her physical appearance. But by the end, when they asked her whether it was acceptable for a priest to be sexy, she answered,

"Yeah!" And when they asked, "Do you feel like you can be this girl and a priest?" she replied with confidence, "Yes, I *am* this woman and a priest . . . I can see myself as those things together and I think before I was trying too hard to either separate them, or hide one or hide the other, and now I don't have to hide any of it . . . I can be a strong, beautiful, feminine priest all at once."[1]

We responded to this by shouting an enthusiastic "Amen!" and, with a renewed sense of purpose, went back to writing.

Even amid the frustrations of ministry—and there are many—we hope that this book inspires others, just as the stories of Emily and hundreds of other young clergy have inspired us.

Acknowledgments

We want to thank first and foremost the many pastors who trusted us with their stories and allowed us to include them in this book. We are grateful for your ministries and hope that this is an accurate and helpful testimony. This book would not exist without you.

We also wish to thank Susan Olsen, convener of the Young Clergy Women Project, and the board and members of the Young Clergy Women Project for their support and vision in creating a new space for young clergy women all over the world.

Thanks to the staff at Chalice Press and to the amazing friends, family members, and colleagues who supported us and took the time to read and edit this book: Kelli Blakeney, Hannah Brown, Brianna Burnett, Margaret Burnett, Mary Button, Jason Byassee, Bill Davis, Wendy Dewberry, Cat Dodson, Ian Doescher, Sarah Edgecombe, Miguel Angel Escobar, Lynne Frech, Mary Newberg Gale, James Goodlet, Kendra Hotz, Jac Klassen, Julie Chamberlain Sipe McDonald, Joshua Robinson, Jenny Sharrick, Sarah Stoneking, Rachel Thompson, Talae Tuitele, Sarah Wiles, and Betsy Braden Wood. Additionally, thank you to Emily Bloemker, Chuck Campbell, Anna Carter Florence, Donna Schaper, and Vicki Weinstein for reading and endorsing this book, and a very special thank you goes to John Shorb for serving as our wonderful editor. All of these people have been sources of great encouragement and insight during the writing process.

Many thanks to our colleagues, friends, and support network at Second Presbyterian Church in Indianapolis, Indiana, especially Richard Baker, David Berry, Lewis Galloway, Bob Hunter, Karen Lang, Shelle Louer, Pat Shirey, Ruth Twenty, Erin Benedict, and the Lake Fellows. Thanks to the Church Health Center for their patience and enthusiasm and to our friends and colleagues at First Presbyterian Church of Clarion,

Pennsylvania, and Montreat Conference Center for all their love and for providing such a fabulous "place set apart"[1] for writing and renewal.

Thanks to the restaurants for providing food, caffeine, and adult beverages on those occasions where we needed some spirits for inspiration, especially Medici's on 57th and Park 52 in Chicago, Brougge and Café Patachou in Indianapolis, and Otherlands Coffee in Memphis.

We would like to thank Facebook for assistance in time management, networking, and procrastination.

And finally, we want to thank Reggie Weaver for enduring this writing process from the beginning and for reminding folks that no matter what the haters say, "You'll be all right, fella."

Bless her heart. Phrase, Southern. [bles hur HAHRT]
Variations: *Bless his heart. Bless your heart.*

1. Phrase used to justify saying something impolite
   Example 1: "Bless her heart, her outfit sure is . . . creative."
   Example 2: "She has never showed up for a meeting on
       time in her life, bless her heart."
2. Phrase used to express concern, love, or sympathy
   Example 1: "Bless your heart, I know how stressful that
       can be."
   Example 2: "I've been there. Bless her heart."

Introduction

For many professional pastors, the road to ordination begins in a seminary. We spend three, or six, or twelve years preparing for our ministerial future through academic study, internships, chaplaincy, and reflection. To their credit, many seminaries do their best to take seriously the role of women in the church and to address critical women's issues in the church—if for no other reason than the increasing number of women attending seminary.

But then our seminary education is over, and we move into a whole new world: the church. Navigating the church as young women in ministry can be both challenging and rewarding, but in either case, our experiences in the church can quickly show us there are some lessons we should have learned in seminary that they never got around to teaching us. In many denominations, women have only been allowed to serve in ordained ministry for a few years, and some churches still forbid women from serving in their denomination. Even among churches who have embraced women's leadership for years, many congregations are simply not used to seeing a woman in the role of pastor. They can be shocked at our presence, just as we are shocked at their responses to us.

The uniqueness of our callings means that we continue to forge new paths for women. Even now, when women have been in the "church" force for many years, we still encounter situations where no woman has ever gone before. For young pastors in the first few years of ministry, these new situations

1

may be amplified: Our congregations may have never seen a pregnant pastor before, or seen a female officiate a wedding, or done their premarital counseling with a single woman. Young women in ministry are often presented with new challenges, some similar to the ones our mothers in the faith first faced and some that have a distinctively twenty-first-century feel.

Moreover, for many of us, our first ordained position is often our first job. While the "second career" ministers bring a wealth of experience and knowledge to their ministries, many young pastors have spent only a limited amount of time working a full-time job. A study done by the Presbyterian Church (USA) found that almost 30 percent of newly ordained female pastors had no full-time employment experience prior to their ordination, and well over 50 percent had less than five years of work experience before they were ordained.[1] With those statistics, some of the realities in the workplace are likely to blindside us. We've probably never thought too much about retirement plans, management styles, or what it actually feels like to moderate committee meetings. Try as they might, our seminaries cannot fully prepare us for the tangible realities of full-time, professional ministry in any setting, regardless of our gender or age. We stumble through these lessons, seeking support from our colleagues in ministry and hoping that at least one of them is within a reasonable driving distance.

The good news is that we seem to be pretty good at what we do. Clergy tend to be more stressed and less healthy than people in other professions,[2] but women seem to handle these challenges better than men. One study puts it this way:

> Researchers found that women had much less role ambiguity than their male counterparts. Female ministers demonstrated a better sense of understanding of what they needed to do in their vocation and how to accomplish it than their male colleagues. Clergy women also appeared to have fewer problems in setting limits with others, reported greater cognitive coping skills,

and suffered less stress from feelings of being trapped in conflicts than did males.[3]

Yet even with our skills, we may find less happiness in our ministries due to the unique challenges we face. The recent National Congregations Study says that women in ministry "are less likely to report satisfaction with their jobs than their male colleagues," and "even within denominations that ordained women for decades, many congregations are still reluctant to hire women as their main clergy person."[4]

Young clergy women struggle with the unique pressures that all clergy—young and old, male and female—face each and every day. But what makes life as a young clergy woman unique is the combination of living into what we envision our young lives to be while living into who we are as clergy. It is officiating a funeral on the same day as we get our first mammogram and preaching on the Magnificat when we are eight months pregnant. It is trying to figure out if a minister can have a boyfriend or how your spouse fits in at the church. Perhaps our uniqueness is simply the combination of being young, female, and clergy.

These surprising realities are all too common for many young women entering ministry. Nobody ever told us that crossing our legs or wearing sandals could make or break our careers. Yet most female pastors have stories like these—small, everyday occurrences that can sour a meeting. Get a group of us together, and you will be amazed at the stories you hear: stories of anger, angst, and insensitivity, juxtaposed with the powerful moments of witness that remind us why we are called into this ministry in the first place. Collecting these stories has been cathartic and heartening, and we wanted to assemble our experiences in a way that lifts our hearts, heals our brokenness, and gives voice to the myriad of experiences that await us in our callings.

Bless Her Heart takes seriously the stories and experiences of young clergy women. It challenges us to prepare for life in the parish and offers practical reflections on how we can plan for real-life situations ahead of us. It does this by embracing the ancient tradition of women's truth telling. Women have shared their lives with each other at the well, at the sewing circle, at the beauty shop, and on the Internet. When we offer our common experiences to our sisters, we find it possible to honor the beauty, lament the pain, and with the support of each other, live to do it all the next day. So each chapter offers two first-person stories that testify to both the absurd and the glorious parts of ministry. They are told from the perspective of a young clergy woman and are all true accounts from friends and colleagues. The details have been changed, but the stories themselves reflect the experiences of women in all different kinds of ministries, and in different Christian traditions.

Each chapter will then name the issue and outline the situation at hand. This gives a glimpse into what ministry often looks like for many young professional women. We break down the story and describe the practical, day-to-day situations that many young women face. We will explore practical questions about the pastor's Sunday schedule, women's options for clerical vestments, and etiquette during a particularly difficult hospital meeting. This "naming" also presents a chance to empathize with women who may have had similar experiences to yours, and taking a cue from scripture, engage in a little literary lamentation.

While we acknowledge the absurdity and frustration of many of these stories, we also believe that we are engaged in the most meaningful work imaginable. On our best and worst days, we continue to cherish, honor, and embrace the work of ministry. So in the second half of each chapter, we reframe each particular experience by looking at the issues through the lens of scripture. The reframe is our attempt to see if we can find deeper meaning in the names we are given each and every day. The conclusion of each chapter also offers a chance for truth telling in the form of a story or anecdote. But these stories will portray women in ministry who are taking the everyday frustrations in stride—not by pretending they don't exist, but by using their faith to find meaning in the chaos.

Not all of these situations will apply to you. Depending on your denomination, calling, age, or location, you will most certainly find yourself considering things that you haven't experienced or that you disagree with. You may not be a young clergy woman yourself but someone considering seminary, navigating the pressures of ordination, working with a young clergy woman, or trying to date one. Our goal is not to say that this is how it is for *every* young female pastor but to say that these stories and experiences are *some* aspect of the truth for many, and there are friends to be found and lessons to be learned when we share them with each other. Moreover, these chapters are not an attempt to defend unreasonable actions or comments, nor are they a chance to defame the ministerial calling. Instead, we wish to witness them with each other in the hopes that we will gain strength, insight, and practical wisdom from the experiences of others. It is our hope that you will come away from this book with an energized spirit for ministry, drawing on the wisdom of scripture and fellowship with other pastors.

Bless Her Heart asks the questions that keep us up on Saturday night and make us think twice about stepping into the pulpit on Sunday morning. By sharing our stories, our lessons, and our passions, we hope that a newer generation of young clergy women will be awakened and energized by the sacred absurdities of life in ministry.

1

Pedicures for the Pastor

Issues with Shoes and Sandals

Funny that a pair of really nice shoes make us feel good in our heads—at the extreme opposite end of our bodies.

—LEVENDE WATERS

You wouldn't really think that shoes would come first. With all the issues and challenges of ministry, are feet, shoes, and toenail polish really the number one frustration? Yet a significant number of women mentioned this challenge and had a crazy story to share. For some reason it would seem that our feet are of great interest. Perhaps it's because of our congregations: Sometimes the only thing they notice about our appearance in worship is our shoes, since that's the only thing not covered by a robe or alb. Perhaps it's because *we* are a little preoccupied with our flats, heels, wedges, boots, peep-toe pumps, and summer sandals. Perhaps it's a preoccupation of the pastors we work with: One woman said that after her first Sunday on the job, the pastor called her into the office and said, "The most important thing to remember is to always wear black shoes. Other than that, you were fine."

When leading worship, pastors often cover up their clothes with a long robe or alb. The thinking here is that this enables the congregation to focus on the Word and worship rather than on the pastor's clothes or body. It also serves to differentiate the pastor from the members of the congregation and to recall the long history of robe-wearing apostles. The trick, however, is that the robe doesn't descend to the floor. People will see our shoes, so we have to ask a seemingly simple question: What shoes will we wear? Our choices speak to our sensibility and style while leaving us open to the fashion judgments of others. We have to think intentionally about what we communicate in worship, which in some cases can include our choices of footwear.

However we learn the lessons of clergy footwear, it is often the first challenge that many young women face, and silly as it may seem, it is often formidable, confusing, and a ripe subject for the miniscandals of daily church life.

Running the Sunday Race

I barely got the kids out the door in time to preach the early service a few weeks ago. Our whole family was exhausted from the weekend, and I was sore from running my first 5K on Saturday. However, I managed to get everyone clean, dressed, and out the door with fifteen minutes to spare. That alone was enough to make Sunday a holy and sacred day.

After preaching and teaching a Sunday school class, my feet and calves were aching in my classic black Nine West pumps. I figured some Advil would help, so I grabbed some and went off to the next service. As I was reading the New Testament lesson, I decided I couldn't stand my preaching shoes any longer. So as I began my sermon, I simply stepped out of my shoes to give my feet some room to stretch and breathe while I stood for twenty minutes. The service continued, the choir sang a fabulous anthem, and all was well.

In my case ignorance was bliss for four days. But finally, someone brought my offense to light. One of the other pastors came to my office, looking concerned, and said she wanted me to know that, on the previous Sunday, she saw me step out of my shoes.

I know I must have stared blankly at her for a good fifteen seconds before responding, "Oh?"

"Yes." She continued. "And I just thought I would let you know, in case some congregation members saw the same thing I saw."

As what she was saying began to sink in I couldn't help thinking, "Is this what you noticed in worship? Really? My feet? Not the scripture or sermon or even the music, but my feet?" I thought it might ease her mind if she knew *why* I stepped out of my shoes. I told her about the 5K I ran that Saturday and how sore my feet were after standing for hours Sunday morning in heels. When she remained expressionless and did not respond, I elaborated a bit more on my aching feet and calves, but it was to no avail. I had clearly committed a social faux pas, and the rationale behind it was irrelevant. So with all the charm I could muster, I replied, "Well, thank you for letting me know."

What difference did this make to our worship? What is it about having sore feet and standing in heels all morning that is so fascinating and conversation worthy? Am I truly the only pastor with tired feet?

Let's go out on a limb here and say, no, you are not the only one with sore feet. As women we are called into ministry with all that makes up who we are. We live into our gifts and our calling with all of our femininity and aim to be authentic leaders, bringing the depths of ourselves to the work and the people that

God places before us. With that responsibility comes a good deal of running around and, with that, some significant and fancy footwork. If we believe that our whole selves are charged with the pastoral calling, then we acknowledge the gifts and stresses of the bodily limbs that haul us around. Moreover, everyone has tired feet, including the other pastor in this story. As clergy, what makes our feet so special that someone should take notice?

God calls pastors into a social spotlight. Other people in public professions share this responsibility and are seen as a representative of a business or of the state. No matter how much we encourage lay leadership, pastors are seen as representatives of the church, and even a representative of God. This can and should make most of us a little nervous. Moreover, young clergy women may serve as representatives of various groups and subsets of the population. To our churches, we may represent the young adults and future of the church and are seen as a source of wisdom to the question, "Why aren't youth and young adults coming to church?" We are representative of young women, the daughters and granddaughters and mothers and sisters of the people in the pews. Thankfully, when we stand before a congregation for the call to worship, we never stand alone, as God is always standing with us. But so are the thoughts, prayers, expectations, and preoccupations of our congregations. Many church members look to us to model honesty and holiness, care and communication, sacrifice and spiritual depth. Therefore, what supports us and holds us up—literally, what shoes we wear—can be a topic of great interest and discussion in the life of the congregation.

Young clergy women need strong systems of support to hold us up, which include our shoes. Perhaps the common Sunday routine can shed some light as to why it is so important to have good support. Some of us begin our work in multiple services, in addition to speaking with and offering pastoral care to church members. Participating in worship is one of the greatest honors and one of the most exhausting gifts of ministry. It is a wonderful privilege to stand and face the flock you love and lead them in praising God, prayers, proclaiming the Word, and declaring them forgiven, graced, and unconditionally loved. Yet it is exhausting, emotionally and physically, to lead worship, especially when standing for hours in uncomfortable shoes and a hot robe.

In addition to serving in the morning service, many of us also teach at least one class before or after a worship service. We make a quick change from our robe to our Sunday clothes to be the teacher and facilitator of Christian education. Sometimes we are standing in front of the lecture podium; sometimes we are sprawled out on the floor of the children's room playing Abraham and Sarah with three-year-olds. We teach, discuss, and explore God's Word together as a community of believers. We pray with and for each other, discuss the topic for the next Sunday, run the halls, organize the volunteers, fix the problems—and then everyone disperses to the coffee and donuts. Everyone except the pastor, that is. We run by the restroom, speak to folks in the hallway, put our robes back on, check our makeup, get a microphone, glance at the bulletin, and get back to the sanctuary for the worship service. And our feet, encased in our lovely Sunday shoes, bear the brunt of this running, leaping, and juggling.

Then there are the summer months. In case you forgot, it's hot and humid in the summer, and bless your heart if you are in a congregation without air conditioning. And in wool or wool-blend clerical garb, it's just plain sweaty. No matter how light our clothes are underneath, or how *little* we wear underneath, it's hot in the chancel, especially with all our responsibilities illuminated under the bright lights. So the obvious choice, and the choice many female members of the congregation make, is to wear sandals. Now you probably don't wear your sassy sandals without cute toenails and exfoliated feet, and it would make sense to pick a fun summer color for our toes. We are still women, after all. Why would a clergy woman get a pedicure on a day off and when asked, "What color would you like?" respond with, "Something that is subtle and chancel appropriate." Yet for some folks in our congregation, the running, the shoes, and the toenails can be an issue.

Finally, let's be honest: Dressy, pointy, high-heel Sunday shoes are rarely both fashionable *and* functional. Many of the heels are wide enough for us to maneuver the steps to the chancel and the processional down the long aisle, but the toes of the heels are very square or very pointy. Our feet get cramped in our shoes, but if we are able to stand without falling, it's all worth it.

No matter what your week looks like, Sunday mornings can seem more rushed and more chaotic than other workdays. And sometimes our Sundays are not finished at the end of worship. Many churches have evening services, classes, youth group, or Bible study, so pastors are asked to spend the entire day leading the congregation. Therefore, more often than not, Sundays are not days of rest for clergy—male or female—and not all congregation members comprehend this reality. So by Monday morning, our feet are especially tired. We may or may not spend our Saturdays at a 5K, but the Sunday routine can leave our feet and our bodies completely exhausted.

Standing Barefoot on Holy Ground

In the midst of the Sunday chaos, we can be reminded that we are not the only ones who have foot problems. Throughout the Hebrew and Christian Scriptures, there are plenty of examples of messengers of God whose lives are profoundly impacted by God's claim on their lives—and it seems that even the feet of these prophets get tired. The scriptures tell us of God's people who are weary and need to rest their feet. And with footrest comes shoe rest. Scripture tells us to take off those shoes, and when we are faced with yet another race to run, we can turn to scripture to give us some very practical advice about our feet.

If we think theologically about sandals, the first person who comes to mind is Moses. When God appears to Moses through the burning bush, God commands Moses to take off his sandals since he is standing on holy ground. Moses is probably shocked by this experience, but he manages to follow these simple directions and take off his sandals. Then as Moses hears and obeys God's command, he puts his sandals back on and proceeds on his journey to declare that "I AM" sent him to lead God's people out of slavery. Moses, with incredible faithfulness, puts on his sandals, walks away from the holy ground, and declares the will, hope, and passion of "I AM" to the Israelites.

Moments of standing on holy ground happen for all of us throughout our ministry, and if we are looking for opportunities to see them, Sunday morning is a particularly good place to start. God calls us to pay attention, to look around, to not be so consumed in the details of our days that we miss the burning bushes right in front of us. We might find one short moment when we can truly pray. Yet this moment can be a burning bush for us, a time when we can take off our sandals, figuratively or literally. Once in a while we stumble into a deep and enriching scripture lesson with the children of the church. We forget about the performance of worship and get carried away by the message and music. We offer someone some honest and rewarding pastoral care and receive the gift of knowing that we are helping out a fellow traveler. We may even find a moment when we can receive care and support offered to us. Each of these moments is a burning bush, telling us to stop for a moment and breathe in the awe of God's power. When faced with those moments, we are called to remove our sandals, in whatever way we can, and stand, even for just a moment, on holy ground.

God calls us to stop, take off our sandals, and listen. Then when we catch our breath, we take a cue from Moses and put those sandals back on. We go back out into the world to proclaim that "I AM" wants to liberate the oppressed, heal the broken, and be known in this world. It may seem strange to our congregation; we may even get comments from other pastors or e-mails from the Bible studies asking us why we would take our shoes off. But by removing our shoes, we recognize the importance of the moment and opportunity we have as pastors. Standing barefoot on holy ground may elicit some stares, but by removing our sandals we remember the beauty and awe of the moment, using that as energy to go off in search of the next one.

Anointing Our Feet

Perhaps the most intimate of all "feet" experiences in scripture is Jesus washing the feet of the disciples. The gospel of John captures this moment in a classic Johannine way: Jesus says something to the disciples, which is completely misunderstood, and then he has to explain himself once again. In this case, it is Simon Peter who misses the point of the foot-washing action. Feet, it seems, are not enough for Peter:

> [Jesus] came to Simon Peter, who said to him, "Lord, are you going to wash my feet?" Jesus answered, "You do not know now what I am doing, but later you will understand." Peter said to him, "You will never wash my feet." Jesus answered, "Unless I wash you, you have no share with me." Simon Peter said to him, "Lord, not my feet only but also my hands and my head!" (Jn. 13:6–9)

Ordinarily, we might think that Peter makes a good point. Jesus *does* need to prepare our hands and our heads for the work of ministry. We must be willing to think wisely and tangibly—that is, with our heads and our hands—about the tasks of ministry.

Yet Jesus' actions are not only about cleansing the disciples. He knows well that the road he will soon walk will head directly for a cross. Jesus' final walk is full of pain and suffering but so too are the walks the disciples will face. Their walks—literally, their feet—will bear the marks of loneliness, danger, and hopelessness. In the days and months following Jesus' death on the cross, the disciples will desperately want to plant their feet on solid and supportive ground. They will seek refuge wherever they can find it: in each other, in denial, in preaching, and in the resurrection. By anointing them for their future—by washing their feet—Jesus not only prepares himself for the coming sacrifice but also prepares his friends for the futures that await them. Giving of himself to the disciples at the end of his earthly life, Jesus gently anoints his friends one last time and instructs them that they are to do the same for others.

When we take the time to care for our feet we should remember this simple and loving act performed by Jesus in his last few hours. Our preoccupation with pedicures, toenail polish, and footwear can be thought of as an anointing, giving us opportunity to recall how Jesus has prepared us for the task ahead. Our own walks will include times of joy and suffering, but as children of God and ministers in the church, we are anointed for a holy purpose. With even the slightest care of our weary feet, we can remind ourselves of our God who cleanses, exfoliates, and polishes the servant's feet, holding us up and sustaining us on the journey.

Cajun Shrimp

Our Sunday schedules will continue to be stressful, and our feet will continue to grow weary. Yet in the midst of running the race, we can take comfort in the spiritual "Guide My Feet" that says, "Guide my feet while I run this race, for I don't want to run this race in vain!"[1] No matter what kinds of looks we get from our congregation, we can remove our sandals when we find a holy moment, and we can care for ourselves by anointing our feet in any way we see fit. The foot frustrations and shoe situations will more than likely follow us around, but we can take refuge in a God who provides for us in the midst of the journey:

> After participating in three Sunday morning worship services, I greeted a few dozen people and listened to the joys and concerns of some members in our congregation. I hung my robe up in the sacristy, wondered when it was last dry cleaned, and returned to my office exhausted. I wrote a few sticky notes of upcoming surgeries as reminders to myself for later that week.
>
> Now I know better, but for some reason I decided to check my e-mail before leaving the office for a few hours.

Among other things, there was an e-mail from one of the women I had spoken with that morning. She had shared concerns about her grandchild, so I opened the e-mail to see if there was something else going on. But to my surprise, it was not about her grandchild at all. She had sent me an e-mail entirely about my sandals. No, more specifically, she sent me an e-mail about my toenail polish! She let me know that she did not approve of my red toenail polish, or my open-toed sandals, or that I wore both with my robe in worship. She said that it is just not appropriate for pastors to have brightly painted toenails at all—however, she conceded, my fingernails should be manicured more often and should always have a clear coat, or even better yet, a French manicure.

As I sat, stunned and staring at my computer, I read her e-mail a second time and then again a third. By then I was fuming. How dare she send me an e-mail about my sandals or my toenail polish? Why does she need to express her opinion about my nail regimen? And more important, how in the world does the color of my toenails affect the thirty minutes I had just spent listening to her and all the times I had been there for her in the past?

I let her e-mail reside in my in-box for a few days as I tried to think of a brilliant, yet pastoral, response. I thought of a few brilliant ones, but none of them was anywhere near pastoral, and some were barely polite. So I decided not to respond at all.

I saw her again and again, supported her through various times of her life, and was increasingly convinced that my red toenails did not damage our relationship in the least. She continued to trust me with the deep pains and great celebrations of her life. I continued to minister with her, and our relationship remained strong and positive. So either she was only venting that Sunday afternoon and my toenails really weren't a big deal, or she got all of her personal opinions out in that e-mail, and that was enough satisfaction for her.

Sometimes I get a little preoccupied with my shoes, and I think, "What is the congregation thinking of me?" But it seems to me that wearing what I want to wear and being myself on Sunday morning is important. The more I do that, the more I can model for my congregation how they can be themselves in the midst of difficult situations. Maybe that has helped this woman with the problems in her life. Maybe not. But either way, I continue to love her and continue to have my toenails painted with the various bright and seasonal OPI colors. Currently my favorite color is "Cajun Shrimp."

2

I Know You Are, but What Am I?

Establishing Pastoral Identity

I've grown certain that the root of all fear is that we've been forced to deny who we are.

—FRANCES MOORE LAPPE

It's hard enough to be a young woman. Our twenties and thirties are a complicated time of decision making, planning, moving, and generally attempting to get our stuff together. In his book *After the Baby Boomers: How Twenty- and Thirty-Somethings Are Shaping the Future of American Religion*, sociologist Robert Wuthnow writes,

> In the 1970s . . . developmental psychologists argued that people pretty much established their adult

identity during their late teens and were already fully formed adults by their twenty-first birthday . . . That was a view of the typical life cycle that made sense in the 1950s or 1960s but it no longer makes sense today.[1]

Instead, we are staying in school longer, working more, getting paid less, marrying later, traveling, volunteering, learning, and becoming—or, at least, feeling like—an "adult" at a much later time in life.

Just when we think that we might have gotten some traction on finding out who we are as young women, we tack on the pressures of ordained ministry. With that, all of those "becoming" questions have an additional layer of stress spread across them. If you were struggling with pressures of relationships before, how much are those struggles heightened by a congregation that expects you to get married but not to date? Or one that wants you to live in the neighborhood when you clearly can't afford it? Establishing our individual identities is a lifelong process, yet as women, we know that there are certain biological, social, and economic factors that require us to *move along*. When we add "pastor" to the list of identities, we can feel lost and confused— while at the same time, trying to provide comfort, guidance, and peace to a community of faith.

When we say "young clergy women," what do we mean? Are we young first, clergy second, and women third? Are we some Trinitarian version of all three, each of us independent and yet each entirely the whole? Are we required to put parts of ourselves on the shelf in certain situations, or can we be all that we are without trying to be all things to all people? Establishing pastoral identity is not just about growing into our authority in the pulpit. Our pastoral identities are wrapped up in our careers, joys, vision, femininity, sexuality, maternity, morality, and humanity. What does it mean to be young . . . and clergy . . . and a woman?

The Collar of Doom

I was two years into my first call when I was asked to lead a group of high-school students on a week-long mission trip to Uganda. Our mission volunteer from the church was to go ahead of us to get things ready for our visit, so I was left to shepherd a dozen high schoolers on two international flights, through customs, into Entebbe, and to our mission partners in a rural area of the country. Before we left, the volunteer suggested that I wear my clerical collar on the flight. I looked young, almost the same age as the teenagers I was accompanying, so wearing the collar would show the airport officials that I was a pastor. We would have a much easier time getting in and around the country, he suggested, if we looked like a church group.

Of course, this request presupposed that I *had* a collar. Clerical collars had not really been my favorite thing in seminary or in the church. I had never even met or seen a female pastor until I went to seminary, and I had certainly never seen a woman wearing a collar. I thought they seemed antiquated, uncomfortable, and masculine. I hated the idea that as a young woman, I needed to assert my pastoral identity with an article of clothing that, for the last several centuries, had been reserved for male priests. Honestly, the collar freaked me out. So rather than get derailed by it, I simply avoided it. I preached on Sunday, I visited the hospitals, I worked for social justice, I did all the things pastors do, and I felt and acted just like the ordained minister I was. I really had no major problems with my pastoral identity. I aimed to show people that I was a pastor by my words and actions, not by my clothes.

But now the collar was necessary. So I summoned my courage and bought one. When it came in the mail, I put the thing on and stood in front of the mirror. I felt traumatized and immediately burst into tears. I didn't look anything like me; I did not know who this person was. All the fears and insecurities that had been patiently lurking in the back of my mind jumped to life with the arrival of this collar. In a flash I thought about my cousin who said women should never preach and the words of Paul stating, "Let women keep silent." I thought about the dreams I had as a child, the expectations of my family, the responsibility of preaching the Word, the centuries of women who had kept their place in the home, the people who had fought for our place in the pulpit, and the people who thought that I was out of place—and me, standing among them in that stupid collar, feeling insecure, inferior, and infuriated with myself. So I ripped the collar off and sought the counsel of my wise and wonderful partner who assured me that I was a fine pastor without black-and-white polyester affixed to my neck.

But I still had to get these teens to Uganda. So against my better judgment, I packed my new collar in my carry-on bag. At the end of the flight, I stepped into the tiny airplane bathroom and put the collar back on. As I stood there shaking, I thought to myself, "I am a twenty-six-year-old woman, I have all these teenagers in a foreign country, and the success of our trip rests on whether or not I can bear the weight of this collar." I took a deep breath and said a prayer, and we made it through customs. As soon we got to our mission site, I took the collar off and vowed to never wear it again.

That plan lasted about three days. My anticollar intentions were again thwarted by our Ugandan partners when I was asked to preach on Sunday morning. And I was asked to preach about an hour before the worship service started. My panic must have been obvious, because our mission partner leaned over and whispered what he thought were words of comfort: "Don't worry, you'll be fine. Just put on your collar."

In the years since, I still have not found peace with the collar. I have watched other colleagues make the collar theirs. One friend wears a purple collar, one has rhinestones on hers, some people even feel more comfortable in the collar and wear it all the time. For me, it has always been a hindrance rather than a help. The collar is supposed to be a tangible, visible symbol of pastoral authority. It is internationally recognized, it has no boundaries, it gives us identity, and helps others identify us. But it has never worked for me. I do not wear my collar, and I think I never will.

Shaping our pastoral identity is an intentional process. Most seminaries have programs designed to introduce us to the realities of ministry. We complete internships and pastoral education, reflect with other students who are going through the same thing we are, read books on vocation, and are asked to share our "call story" at Bible studies and church dinners. We have very specific language designed to describe this process. We even acknowledge that having a "pastoral identity" indicates we know how important this work is. A pastor stated,

> I work with a lot of young adults who are trying to figure out their vocation, even though they don't call it that. When I am struggling with being a pastor, I remind myself that we have words like "vocation," "call," and "identity" in our vocabulary, and that we have the opportunity to think and write about what kind of pastor we are to be. I routinely find that other people in other professions don't have that. They start out on a professional trajectory and have almost no time to think critically about what they want to do and how they have changed along the way. In my ministry, I am grateful to have that language and try to share it with other people my age.

But for all of our planning and reflecting, our pastoral identity is subject to the random whims of influence that occur during ordinary time in our ministry. Preaching a traumatic funeral, enduring a church scandal, cleaning out a house after a flood, or watching an international tragedy unfold with millions of other people—these are all things that bend and shape us into the people and pastors that we are. These situations come out of nowhere and even the smallest thing—for example, putting on a collar—can have a profound effect on the future of our ministry.

Young clergy women are not the only pastors who find joy and trouble in establishing pastoral identity, and yet our experiences are unique among men and among older women. Men simply do not face the same challenges of identity that women face. For centuries women have been told that they cannot do many things: vote, own property, divorce, work outside the home. In recent years, our modern Western culture has turned the tables on many of these once-forbidden acts. Now instead of debating these issues, they are, to some extent, a given. The same thing is not true for women in ministry. The largest church institutions in the world, and the largest in our country, do not permit the ordination of women to ministerial office. Our mothers in the faith worked tirelessly for many years to change this reality and give us the opportunities to serve in ordained ministry. Yet for many of them, this dedicated struggle is what defined their ministry. They wrote the classic texts on patriarchy and feminism and endured harsh ridicule each and every time they stepped into the pulpit. As young women, grateful and indebted to them, we enjoy a tenuous freedom in which we can ask whether or not women's ordination is what will define and shape our pastoral identity.

This means that as women in ministry, we still have to explain and defend our pastoral identity. We might have to defend ourselves while trying to define ourselves. We are often reminded that in places very close to us, just around the corner, we have barely stepped within the door or are not allowed at all. As the woman in the previous story demonstrated, the perceived limits of our gender, our age, and our experience take a toll on us whether we like it or not. One pastor said,

I am great at some aspects of ministry, and not so great at others. Claiming my ministerial identity in part has to do with improving my weak spots and accepting my limitations—while living with folks who think I should be good at everything.

Even if we feel completely secure in the ministerial calling, prepared and ready for whatever pastoral emergency comes along, we should feel free to admit that our insecurities pop up at the most unhelpful times, and we can quickly find ourselves shaking in the airplane bathroom.

Moreover, God calls us to discern our precarious pastoral identity in the midst of a drastically changing Christian context. As churches evolve from street-corner denominations to global fellowships, we have to acknowledge that the identity of the church is changing and evolving, just as ours is. Whatever we thought our ministry would look like a few years ago, we have to make room for the notion that the church changes just as we do, and what was essential in our youth may be irrelevant now. One woman said,

> I used to think that I knew the path my ministry would take. It would pretty much be the same path that other professional ministers had taken—college, seminary, church, bigger church, maybe a PhD somewhere along the way. If I was good enough, I might end up in the "Great Preachers" club and maybe even get elected to some important post. But now, with churches closing and new ministry models popping up all the time, I wonder if any of that will really *be* my ministry. Will the church in my future look anything like the church now? Am I really just in this to make money at a big church somewhere—and if I am in it for the money, I think I should have picked another career.

Living into our pastoral identities means that we have to find ways to be the young women we are, called by God into a complicated yet liberating ministry. No one can tell us how to do this, just as no one can tell us when to get engaged, if we should have a child, or where we should plan to live. Nevertheless, these things are issues that most women face, and we have to find ways to be who we are within our complexity.

I'm Only a Child

In order to live into this new identity, we can look to the book of Jeremiah for comforting words of assurance and affirmation of our callings. In the first chapter we are told about a prophet, a young prophet, whom God appointed to speak to the nations on God's behalf:

> The word of the Lord came to me, saying, "Before I formed you in the womb I knew you, before you were born I set you apart; I appointed you as a prophet to the nations." "Ah, Sovereign Lord," I said, "I do not know how to speak; I am only a child." But the Lord said to me, "Do not say, 'I am only a child.' You must go to everyone I send you to and say whatever I command you. Do not be afraid of them, for I am with you and will rescue you," declares the Lord. Then the Lord reached out his hand and touched my mouth and said to me, "Now, I have put my words in your mouth. See, today I appoint you over nations and kingdoms to uproot and tear down, to destroy and overthrow, to build and to plant." (Jer. 1:4–10)

When Jeremiah is nervous, and even in denial, God doesn't let him off the hook. Instead, God tells Jeremiah that he is to go wherever God sends him and speak whatever God tells him to speak. Of course God does not ask Jeremiah to do this without also promising that he will not be alone or harmed. It is both encouraging and terrifying to read what God told Jeremiah he was called to do: "uproot and tear down, to destroy and overthrow, to build and to plant." These are not easy or comfortable tasks that can be done in the morning before going to pick the kids up from school or that can be put on the church calendar or discussed in a weekend retreat. These are the please-get-somebody-else-to-do-it-I'm-too-tired-and-scared tasks. God calls Jeremiah to preach of an entirely new world. And he is called to this immense and incredible task while also embracing his youth.

When we hear God's calling, paired with Jeremiah's response, we find the same spirit of dedicated unease in our callings. In the midst of questions about our age, gender, or clerical status, we are first and foremost called into partnership with the Holy Spirit, to hold the "sighs too deep for words" (Rom. 8:26) and articulate the joys that cannot be contained. We are called to preach and protest, care and commune, yet none of these can be done on a specific time frame, and none of these can be done alone. God calls us with the promise that God will never leave us. While we may offer our Jeremiah-like arguments about being young, being female, being mothers, and being wives, God continues to call us out of ourselves to do God's work of cultivation and growth. Our identities as young and clergy and women will continue to be formed, yet we are assured that our future is in the hands of a God who promises, "I know the plans I have for you. Plans to prosper you and not to harm you. Plans to give you hope and a future" (Jer. 29:11).

Something New

When we try to reconcile two different identities into one, sometimes we find that it is indeed possible. However, other times we realize that it simply cannot be done. Joan Chittister says, "I cannot be what I was before but I can be–in fact I must be–something new."[2] With these words in mind, we can look again to Moses as a helpful model. Moses grew up as an Israelite in Pharaoh's household. Although we don't know too much from scripture about his childhood with Pharaoh, we can infer that it was a nice one and that, although he was nursed by his Hebrew mother and might have known that he was an Israelite, he adapted pretty well to his posh surroundings. For

Moses, being Hebrew and being Egyptian were, at least for a time, a coexistent identity.

Then something happens that brings the incongruity to light:

> One day, after Moses had grown up, he went out to his people and saw their forced labor. He saw an Egyptian beating a Hebrew, one of his kinsfolk. He looked this way and that, and seeing no one he killed the Egyptian and hid him in the sand. (Ex. 2:11–12)

In this moment, Moses saw the forced labor of his people for the first time. He was enraged, most certainly at his Egyptian counterparts and also possibly at himself for neglecting the Israelites from his place of power in Pharaoh's home. In his rage, he kills the Egyptian and is forced to flee Egypt, thus beginning his journey from murderer to liberator. Moses becomes a leader, though certainly not the Egyptian ruler he was trained for as the adopted grandson of Pharaoh. He becomes the leader of his oppressed people and leads them out of slavery. When he finally "saw" the forced labor of the Israelites, he realizes he cannot be the powerful Egyptian he was before. He must be something new.

Growing up and growing into our ministries as pastors can be painful and challenging. We cling to our old ways, believing that they somehow give us our identity: Who am I if I am not the party girl? the intellectual? the radical? When we try to change and become something new, how much of ourselves is lost in that transformation? Being a woman and a pastor does not mean that we have to sacrifice our personality, our quirks, or our flair. But it may mean that we simply cannot be who we were before. Our roles and responsibilities necessitate that we adopt a new vision of our personal, professional, and spiritual identity. We cannot be our old selves—woman, child, friend, partner, wife, mother—and simply tack "pastor" on to the end of the list. Yet in remembering Moses, we realize that we can use our histories—both the good and bad parts—to shape a new, dynamic, liberating ministry.

The Wedding That Wasn't

Every minister—male or female, old or young, ordained or not—struggles with his or her identity. Matching the daily struggles of our lives with the immense callings of our faith is no easy task. As young women in ministry, we recognize the unique obstacles that we face and forgive ourselves when we feel lost. We need to stand in the strength of our faith and be aware of the many moments in which our identities shift as we grow. There will be occasions, challenges, and even individuals who attempt to undercut our identities—intentionally or not. When faced with these challenges, we must speak God's word. The form, substance, and very identity of our ministry are strengthened when we simultaneously fulfill our call while facing great challenges.

One of the first times I really felt like a pastor was when I was asked to officiate a wedding. My first church was huge, and the sanctuary was gorgeous, so it was naturally *the* place in town to get married. When we booked a wedding for people who were not church members, the staff protocol was that the service would be assigned to a pastor based on a scheduled rotation. So when the wedding coordinator sent me a quick e-mail on a Friday afternoon asking if I was up for a wedding for a couple from outside the church, I replied that I was definitely available and happily marked it on my calendar.

On the next Monday, I received another e-mail from the wedding coordinator saying that they didn't need me for that wedding. I figured the couple had canceled— either the church, or the wedding entirely—and although I was a little upset, I moved on to the next thing.

It was a few months later when I finally learned what had happened. My colleague mentioned he was doing a wedding that same weekend, and I said casually, "Oh, I was supposed to do a wedding then, but they canceled." He looked at me with huge eyes and then spilled his guts:

This was the same couple whose wedding I was originally scheduled to do. However, they had requested another pastor because they didn't want a woman to officiate their wedding. My colleague went on to say that he felt horrible that he had accepted this wedding and that he was sorry he hadn't told me but that the senior pastor had told him not to. He was conflicted and apologetic; I was furious.

I marched into the senior pastor's office and said through clenched teeth: "We need to talk." I explained everything that was making my blood boil: that they had booked this wedding, even when it went against our church policy of appointing pastors based on a rotation; that they had kept this information from me; that they had intentionally told my colleague to keep it a secret; that they had not defended the standards of our church, which includes the full participation of women in all church matters; and that he seemed to see nothing wrong with the way that he handled the situation. He tried to explain himself but his weak defenses were even more infuriating. I stormed out and didn't speak to any of my colleagues for two weeks.

As I stewed, I realized how much of my pastoral identity was wrapped up in this wedding. To me, that was what a pastor does: They preach on Sunday, visit the hospitals, and do weddings and funerals. To be told that I was unable to experience that because of my gender was devastating. I tried to tell myself that surely there would be other weddings, but this was the first one I was ever asked to do, and the experience of losing that opportunity profoundly affected me. In the end I came back to the church with a spirit of forgiveness and have made amends in my own way. I learned that not only might I disagree with my senior pastor, but he could, on occasion, be wrong. I learned that as pastors, we can do things that are deeply hurtful. I learned that life can be unfair and that I can overreact. I learned that there are wonderful, inspiring ministers worthy of respect and that they are equally unworthy of a pedestal.

However, the most surprising thing I learned was how much of my authority was out of my control. People are going to make decisions for and about me. There will perhaps always be someone who doesn't want me to do their wedding because I am a woman, and there will probably always be some person who will agree with them. But my identity as a pastor is not something that can be taken away. It can be bruised, hurt, or violated—but I am a minister in the Church of Jesus Christ, called by God and blessed by the Holy Spirit. And no wedding, pastor, or protocol can change that.

3

Romancing the Reverend

Singleness, Sex, Divorce, and Dating

> *Dating should be less about matching outward circumstances than meeting your inner necessity.*

> —UNKNOWN

Perhaps you are one of those extremely lucky women who happened to meet their partner before or during seminary. If you are, congratulations! You have managed to avoid some of the most challenging aspects of being a young clergy woman—the intricacies of explaining your job to the hottie at the bar, the terrible trials of online dating, and the almost inevitable question that is, "You're a minister? So can you ever have sex?"

However, you may be one of those rare breeds of women who will seek their soul mate in the midst of what can be a very unsexy profession. You are the one who gets to schedule a date with the understanding that Saturday nights are officially out. You are blessed with the challenge of introducing your significant other to an excited, involved, and perhaps slightly judgmental congregation. And you get to walk the line of responsibility, choice, expectation, and biblical interpretation when considering whether or not sex is an option for you and your potential partner. To you we say, good luck with that!

But the roots of the dating conundrum lie in the same issues of pastoral identity we have already discussed: Who am I? What do I do? How much do I want to share about that with other people? Whether you are partnered, single, or not really looking, any efforts at dating bring up those same identity questions that we ask ourselves in many other situations. However, they can appear much more real when sitting across the bar from someone that you *really like*. Suddenly our identities as ministers become sources of consternation rather than liberation, and we are forced to find a way to talk about our passions without intimidating, shocking, or otherwise freaking out our dates. Even with blind dates, well-intentioned friends, and the subtly constructed dating profile, is there anything trickier than being a single pastor on a date?

The Chaplain of Match.com

I was completely unprepared. My marriage did not fall apart until the second half of my seminary studies, so I put zero, and I mean *zero*, thought into what dating as a single pastor might be like. My first year out of seminary had me negotiating life after divorce, single parenting, and a hospital residency. I rarely came into contact with single men my age nor did I have social venues to meet any.

My first dating foray was online. I tried two websites. It was actually another pastor in my clergy study group who encouraged me to do the online thing because that's where she met her husband. It should be mentioned that her husband was the third person she met. I think she got lucky.

Most men seem intimidated by the fact that we are pastors, but she worked around that by listing her occupation as "working in a nonprofit institution with youth and children." I tried that stance for a while, but I never ultimately felt comfortable about it and found that most men would abandon ship once they found out the "truth." Now four years later, I'm very forthright about my career and parenting responsibilities, which greatly decreases the amount of interest, but it has yielded some crazy results.

My overall experience was that if you claim to be Christian and say that faith is important to you, you are lumped into a conservative group and paired with this type of man. Nothing wrong with those guys, but dates with them often result in heated debates about whether women should be in ministry at all. While interesting theological discussions, they are not so much fodder for dating.

Many men are worried that I will quote scripture or be overly pious, or they think that I don't do enough of this. They see me as a great contradiction—my seemingly liberal political views put up against the perceived conservative bent of my profession. So many self-described atheists or agnostics are attracted to me (and vice versa), but they can't seem to get past my love for that Jesus character.

Then there is the issue of physical attraction and intimacy as a female pastor. A few months ago, a man "winked" at me online, and I thought his profile was a decent match. We began e-mailing back and forth, and in his second e-mail he asked me, "So as a pastor, can you have sex before you get married? Because I'm a man and I have needs that must be fulfilled." He never even asked me my name. I don't know what was more infuriating—that he had the nerve to ask a question like that so quickly or the implication that because I'm a woman and a pastor, I have no sexual needs. I would like to say that this was an isolated incident, but this issue comes up frequently.

I'm sure it's difficult for men to see a female pastor as a sexual being. I jokingly refer to myself as the chaplain of Match.com because as I get to know men, they often relegate me as a friend or someone from whom they seek advice. I actually have a close friend who I met in this way. We chatted and he ended up sharing details about his father's death and his aunt's health problems, and I found myself embodying the same pastoral care role that I do in my church. He has since confessed that while he was initially attracted to me, he now "has too much respect for me to pursue dating." I'm not at all sure what that means.

I continue to hope there really are plenty of fish out there, or at least one, with whom I can be myself. Until I encounter him, I must admit I appreciate the great humor in the oxymoron that is female clergy dating.

Whether you are single or not, and whether or not a similar situation has happened to you, the experience of navigating the dating game can be a microcosm of the larger issues of pastoral identity. As with other issues, our congregation members often like to help out. They attempt to set us up with their grandkids, in-laws, or friends, while at the same time asking us why we can't come to a fall festival on Friday *and* Saturday nights. Most of the time, their efforts are genuine. Like our parents or friends, they want to see us happily partnered up, just as we do. We may even be a little grateful for the extra help. But getting our congregations involved in our dating lives may mean that we have abandoned some much-needed boundaries. And yet, given our schedules, we may ask ourselves, where in the world are we supposed to meet someone *if not* through the church? When it comes to dating, we quickly hit on the issues of professional expectations, boundaries, and time management.

But let's say you happen to meet someone you make a connection with. How then do you plan to address the fact that you are a pastor? If you are fortunate, maybe he or she will just roll with it. But chances are they will be at least a little surprised at your chosen profession and need some room to deal. They will have their own expectations and experiences with clergy, and you will have to figure out when to push and when to let go. One very fortunate pastor said,

> We were on our fourth date, and he still hadn't kissed me. I didn't get it—everything was going so well and I thought he liked me, but maybe we were just going to be friends? I got sick of waiting so finally at the end of the evening I kissed him. He smiled and looked so relieved. He said that he had wanted to kiss me, but he wasn't sure if it was *allowed*. I thought—how many dates were you willing to go on before you found out?

When we meet someone promising, we bump up against these questions of vocation, call, and personal experience. We have to figure out how to share the story of our callings and navigate the implications, giving them room to get to know us as we get to know them.

Let us then assume that things start going well—*very* well. Now we get to ask the Sex Question. Whether or not to do it, when, with whom—these questions can be complicated for women of all ages no matter their profession. But like it or not, clergy women bring a lot of issues to the bedroom. Each of our churches and denominations will have different expectations for us. The Church's views on our sexuality can range from denial and rage to tolerance and enthusiasm. Some of our traditions will have no problems with us dating but draw the line at premarital sex. Some will turn a blind eye, some will assume the best or the worst, and some will worry most about the gender or race of our potential partner or claim that our relationship is a sin. Naturally, all of these preoccupations will influence our actions as well. We may abstain from sex—either outside marriage, commitment, or entirely–or we may decide to jump in when the time is right. We may feel we have to hide what we do from the church, or we may want to celebrate it. Some of us have sex and some of us are virgins–and strangely enough, in the best efforts of both cases, we aim to celebrate God's love for us and care for creation through the celebration and honoring of our bodies. In this part of the dating game, we hit on issues of biblical interpretation, morality, incarnational theology, and ethics, and we navigate all of this while trying to be a positive role model to our own children and teenagers in the youth group.

Perhaps we manage to wade through these waters and find ourselves in a committed relationship with a wonderful person whom we love. Now we must decide, with our partner, how they will or will not be involved in the church community. Will they worship every Sunday or continue going to brunch with their friends? Volunteer with the tutoring program or spend time on their professional work? In certain situations, we may find that, like other things, our spiritual lives grow at different speeds and in different directions than our partners'. And we still have to answer those everyday questions that keep any couple awake at night: bills, kids, jobs, and who took out the trash. The desire to spend time with our beloved and the desire to spend time with those entrusted to our care will always coexist. Sometimes we cancel a meeting to have dinner with our loved one, and sometimes we cancel date night to visit a church member in the hospital. Even in the most solid, loving, committed relationship, issues of pastoral responsibility, community, and stewardship challenge us.

Unfortunately, we may also have to ask the question that none of us, married or single, ever wants to face: What if it doesn't work out? No happy couples like to think about this, and certainly not married couples, but the stresses of our lives can often mean the sacrifice of our relationships. One woman stated,

When my partner and I separated, the larger governing body of our denomination recommended that neither of us share anything with our congregations until our divorce was finalized. Our churches knew nothing, and when I left town, we told them that I had a "family emergency." (If divorce doesn't quality for a family emergency, I sure don't know what does!) So when I left, I was alone to grieve. I was alone with my anger. I was alone *because* we are both pastors. For years, people had flocked to us for care, and when I needed a pastor more than anything, I was alone.

So if you have an ugly breakup, who do you talk to about it? Another female at the church? Or do you leave them all out of it and call your mom or your college roommate? A therapist? A colleague five states away? Struggling with the ups and downs of relationships may mean that we have to engage the questions of pastoral care, grief, and forgiveness. When we are barely staying afloat, we have to again ask the questions of professional boundaries while also remembering the nature of our humanity and the role of pastoral care.

Whether we date men or women, have sex or don't, admit to the blind date that we're a pastor or list "nonprofit employee" on our online profile, being a single, divorced, partnered, or widowed pastor is *hard work*. It means that we have to address the challenging and life-affirming questions about who we are, what we want, and how God is working in our lives. Moreover, we have to be willing to share such challenges with strangers and friends, colleagues and parishioners, in some of the most agonizingly vulnerable ways imaginable—all the while believing and praying that God has someone in mind with whom we can intimately share our ministry, our future, and our life.

Hiding Ourselves

Adam and Eve were made for each other, and lucky for them. But of course, they still managed to get all kinds of things wrong. After eating of the Tree of Knowledge, they both realize their nakedness and hide from God. As the story goes, "But the Lord God called to the man, and said to him, 'Where are you?' He said, 'I heard the sound of you in the garden, and I was afraid, because I was naked; and I hid myself'" (Gen. 3:9–10).

Adam awakens to a knowledge of himself that he is ashamed of. He attempts to hide that truth from God, the one who created him exactly as he is. For this, he is punished, and Adam and Eve are removed from the Garden of Eden. Hiding from God, it would seem, is not a good plan. We might wonder what would have happened if Adam had asked God for forgiveness, if instead of hiding himself he had given of himself openly to God. Could God, who created Adam in his nakedness, have forgiven Adam and welcomed him back? The story doesn't tell us, but it certainly sounds like something God would do. Adam hid his vulnerability from the one who created him to be vulnerable. God does not overlook the irony of this lack of trust and punishes Adam in part because Adam knew who he was and how God had created him—and he actively denied it.

When we awake to our own calls, we may try to hide some parts from God, from others, and from ourselves. Sadly, the challenges of dating seem to necessitate this act. The fear of disclosing our job as a pastor is very real. Many young women simply cannot endure the thought of one more stare, bemused rejection, or theological discussion on a Friday night. When fear and frustration set in, it is tempting to finesse the truth and in some cases this may be necessary and understandable. All of us have to figure out how we tell our own narrative and do it in our own time. One pastor said,

> It was St. Patrick's Day and a bunch of friends from seminary were out at a pub. We were chatting with a group of Irish guys and I struck up a conversation with a lovely guy. After a few green beers, one of his friends finally got around to asking us what we all did for a

living. Now, I usually try to break the news gently, but my friend came right out and said, "We're all pastors!" I thought he was going to faint, and then he just started laughing at us. That was the last thing any of us said to these guys. They pounded their green beers and walked away, laughing to themselves as they moved across the bar. I was humiliated and beyond angry with my friend. Why couldn't she just keep her mouth shut for one night?

Yet dating is an act of openness and vulnerability. We must be willing to show the world our authentic selves, trusting that God has created us to be the beautiful women we are and has redeemed us of all of our sin (including embarrassment and anger), and we must cling to the promises that God will sustain us, even in the midst of an awful date. Hiding aspects of who we are out of fear of rejection often means that we will attract a partner who is only compatible with certain aspects of us. That is no way to share our fearfully and wonderfully made lives with another soul. How and when we disclose our identity is our decision to make, but it is a decision that should not be rooted in shame or fear. Rather, the decisions we make about dating should be rooted in God's promise of unconditional love and in wisdom, trust, and hope.

The Best Sex in Scripture

The Song of Songs, or Song of Solomon, has long been a favorite Bible passage for middle-school boys. But for the single pastors out there, its celebration of physical love bears repeating. No other place in scripture so beautifully describes and celebrates the sensuality of love and sex. As a metaphor for Christ's love for the church or the relationship between God and Israel, Solomon seems to fall a little short.[1] But as a means of honoring the body, the characters in this love poetry can stand up against even the best Harlequin romance novel. The pure joy of love is expressed in this piece of scripture that never even mentions God. Yet scripture, preserved in our tradition for thousands of years and read by middle schoolers from many different cultures, affirms the notion that our sensuality and sexuality are a part of our spirituality.

This does not mean that if we are not sexually active–either by choice, oath, or circumstance–that we are missing out on spiritual growth or knowledge. The realities of Biblical precedent, church politics, and pastoral responsibility mean that every pastor has to define her sexuality. Single clergy, both male and female, make difficult choices about their sexuality. Even married clergy have plenty of sexuality issues to discuss as well. One woman says,

> We were trying to conceive a child, and I took the test on a Sunday morning. It said I was ovulating so I ran to tell this fantastic news to my husband. He replied, "You want to try *now*? You have to preach a sermon today. I can't see you up there in your robe two hours after having sex."

As we tell the young people entrusted to our care, sex is a gift and a responsibility. We as pastors are charged with the incredible task of discerning the wisdom of external pressures that would tell us what we should or should not do, trying to figure out if those pressures are inspired, misguided, or manipulative. But just as God created humans for service and sacrifice, God also created us for joy and pleasure. When it comes to dating, we should feel free to explore the richness of God's creation and celebrate that God has created us with passion, commitment, and freedom.

Awkward Moments

For many reasons, not all of us are in the dating game. When it comes to dating and sex, it can seem like there is nothing easy about being a young clergy woman (it may also seem like there is nothing easy about *dating* a young clergy woman!). Dating can be a microcosm of all the other struggles we face in our ministry. But we cannot deny who we are, in all our complexity, and that we deserve community, companionship, and unconditional love. When we release some of our insecurities, forgive the past transgressions of our former romantic encounters, and open our whole selves to God and to others, we might just find that dating can be a pleasurable, even wonderful, means of enjoying God's plan for our lives.

It took about a year before I was ready to start playing the dating game. I had settled into a new city and my new call as an associate pastor. I tried a few online dating services and was matched with a few guys who appeared to have potential. After one horribly awkward date that ended halfway through dinner, I mustered up enough courage to go out with one more guy the online cupids said would be compatible. Well it turns out, he was not only compatible but amazing. We went on a few dates, talked on the phone, and he had great respect for my commitment to God. He didn't attend church, but he had been raised Christian, and his grandparents still regularly attended. We continued to date and spend more time together but had only been dating about six weeks when the holiday season rolled around.

It goes without saying that the holidays are crazy for pastors, and I feared that I would not get to spend much time with him from Thanksgiving to Epiphany. I was also nervous that he would decide it wasn't very glamorous to date a pastor who doesn't have a free night in December. However, just a few days into my internal frets about our hypothetical holiday breakup, he called to invite me to Thanksgiving dinner at his parent's house. I was beyond giddy yet tried to sound calm and collected on the phone. I had butterflies like a teenager as I debated what to wear to meet the family and wondered what a four-hour road trip with him would look like.

Thanksgiving morning finally arrived. I looked very cute and felt confident that the nice bottle of wine for his mom would be the perfect hostess gift. The road trip was full of good conversation and variety of music. All of my anxieties had completely vanished. We arrived on time and I was introduced to his parents, siblings, and a few cousins. His mom seemed to appreciate the wine and said that we would eat as soon as her parents arrived. I was eating, drinking, laughing, and generally enjoying my fabulous good luck at landing a quality guy with a lovely family who let me be myself and not just the pastor, for at least one holiday event.

And then . . . as we began to take our places around the table, his grandparents came into the dining room. I turned to say hello, and to my horror, I saw that they were not only members of my church, but his grandfather was a deacon! He gave me a strange look, probably because he could tell that the thing I wanted most in that moment was to crawl under the table in the fetal position. The family quickly realized that the grandfather and I knew each other when he gave me a big hug and said that it was quite a surprise to see me at Thanksgiving dinner. And so I enjoyed an enjoyable and yet sufficiently awkward Thanksgiving meal sitting next to my boyfriend and across the table from Deacon Grandpa.

Fortunately, the dinner was wonderful, the family was fabulous, and we all seemed to forget our initial introduction. Because of that, I promised myself that I would not be awkward around his grandparents at church, even if we stopped dating. I have kept that promise . . . and we're engaged.

4

Hemlines and Homiletics

Hair, Makeup, Clothing, and Other Body Issues

On the subject of dress almost no one, for one or another reason, feels truly indifferent: if their own clothes do not concern them, somebody else's do.

—ELIZABETH BOWEN

Nothing gets young clergy women talking more than their clerical clothes. It is almost always a complicated situation, no matter your denomination or the traditions of your church. We may wear different types of vestments, or we may not wear a robe, alb, or stole at all. But what we wear may be a source of conflict for our congregations and for ourselves.

Moreover, we may not make these decisions. We are instructed to wear specific things on these certain days, or we are told that this is the kind of garment we should have. Even when we are asked to dress casually, we often fret over what casual means for us: black pants? collar? jeans? hair up or down? Choosing how we dress can directly affect how people view us in our ministry, and when we take a step in the wrong direction, we tend to hear about it.

Often our comfort in our clothes can influence how comfortable we are with other people. If we don't honor our appearance and exhibit self-confidence, how can we encourage confidence in others? And yet many young clergy women say that sometimes our congregations can be more hurtful than helpful when it comes to our appearance. To that end, we offer the following list.

The Top Ten Most Ridiculous Things Said about Our Appearance

10. "You look so cute up there you could be a news anchor."

9. "Every time you preach all I can think about is what you do—or don't—have on under your robe."

8. "I suggest not wearing that waist sash around your robe. It doesn't really flatter your butt."

7. "Those earrings are too shiny. I couldn't hear your sermon."

6. "You really shouldn't wear your hair in a ponytail in the pulpit. It's unbecoming."

5. "Oh, my . . . your foundation didn't look so cakey from the back row."

4. "You're too pretty to be doing a funeral."

3. "I'm sorry to interrupt you, but you're going to have to move because your legs are going to be a major distraction for me during this meeting."

2. "We've never worried about those vents in the floor, but you're going to get your high heels stuck when you serve communion."

and . . .

1. "You don't look like a minister."

Feel free to add your own favorite comment to this list, because chances are, you've got a good one. And if you don't have one, odds are you will at some point in the near future. It is simply unbelievable what people will say to young clergy women about appearance. Even the most self-confident woman, of any age, will find herself frustrated by the things people actually say out loud.

Perhaps the last one is the most hurtful. "You don't look like a minister," is something said all too often. To their credit, people may not be used to seeing a minister with an eyebrow piercing or knee-high boots. But even pastors who dress more conservatively will get this comment. We may have on our most classic pinstripe suit, and people still assault us with this observation. In most cases they mean no harm, but hearing this over and over again can give one the impression that young clergy women look abnormal or that as women, we are somehow outside the mainstream of the church.

Sometimes this comment is actually meant as a compliment. The same people who have never seen a young female pastor with trendy shoes might be excited by the prospect of one. Women in the congregation might be energized by the idea of a pastor who understands their lives better than others they have met before. Yet even when this is meant to build up rather than tear down, it is difficult to hear day in and day out. It constantly reinforces the idea that we are something other than a normal pastor. One pastor tells of receiving one of these well-intentioned, yet sufficiently awkward, comments after worship. A congregant said to her,

> I really like it when you lead worship because in this congregation we've always had old men as pastors. I just love seeing someone young and fresh who doesn't have gray hair and who still has some energy and life. It's like every Sunday is Youth Sunday now!

The decisions we have to make about our dress can reinforce this idea, as well. Each of us will be asked to answer questions about how we are going to dress as a pastor. When it comes to clerical wear, some options look strikingly similar to the men's vestments. They may or may not be cut specifically for women, but they are often made of the same fabric and offer the same shape. Others are a kind of hybrid between the two: They are made of a lighter material and cut to fit our figure but still evoke the same style. Websites like WomenSpirit.com and ClergyCouture.com offer women's options for clerical garb, with names like the Hildegard, Esther, or Tree-of-Life-with-Sleeves. Some women take it upon themselves to make a robe that fits their style, and some of us can't afford that and get stuck with a robe that's too big, too short, or too worn out. Some of us don't have an option; one pastor said,

> Let's talk about Geneva tabs. They make us wear those at my church. I hate those things. I hate wearing those flaps around my neck, choking me during the sermon and making me feel like a rooster. No wonder guys don't like to wear ties. If they're anything like tabs, I will tell my boyfriend not to wear one ever again.

Whether we inherit a hand-me-down or have it custom made, decide for ourselves what we will wear, or find ourselves at the mercy of a committee, answering the question of if and what kind of clerical garment you will wear can be a daunting process.

Whatever we end up choosing, the physical act of wearing these vestments can be both helpful and difficult for us. Donning a robe for the first time can give us an air of confidence and a visible reminder of the work we are called to do. It can also be completely frightening. A woman dealing with this said,

> I bought a robe several months ago, and it is still hanging in my closet. For some reason, I just can't take it out. That doesn't mean I don't wear *a* robe, because I

borrow one from another pastor just about every Sunday. But for some reason I cannot wear *my* robe. I'm not really sure what that means, but I bet it's not good.

At some point in time, most of us will be asked or even required to wear something that visibly distinguishes us as a pastor. Our experience of that situation will ebb and flow depending on how comfortable we are with our location, our identity, and the garment itself.

Some of us will be asked to forgo the vestments altogether and just find the best attire for the day. This can be even more annoying than finding the right alb, since this means that *each day* you have to pick and choose what looks best. It's like the classic argument of whether or not to wear uniforms to school—are they easier, are they better, or do they fit at all? When it comes to everyday dress, some pastors advise that it is important to look dressy every day, since you never know where the day will lead. Pastors who spend a lot of time in nursing homes might opt to wear a clerical collar, even if their church or tradition doesn't usually wear them. (For people with Alzheimer's or dementia, it can be a comfort to see someone who is obviously a pastor, even if they don't remember who you are or the church you represent.) Another pastor advises that it is always best to visit hospitals looking dressy, since you never know if you might have to talk your way in to see a patient. Yet for women, this can present a challenge. Business suits, pantyhose, and heels every day? It might not be economical, much less comfortable, to plan these outfits for each day. And, truth be told, nothing kills a nice pair of pumps like hospital floors.

Even more fundamental than dress is the underlying question that plagues many women in general: body image. As women, in any profession, body image is something many of us struggle with throughout our lives. We often feel we are too short, too tall, too heavy, too thin or that we have bad skin, bad teeth, bad hair, and so on. We might hear criticism from others, and even criticize ourselves, sometimes without recognizing how hurtful we are being. Just like the comment, "You don't look like a minister" can grow tiring, the constant criticism of our bodies can also have significant emotional, spiritual, and professional effects. One pastor tells this Christmas story:

> I made it home for Christmas after four Christmas Eve services and two flight delays. I had been exhausted since we lit the first candle of Advent and couldn't wait for my grandmother's mashed potatoes and a long winter's nap. I was finally home and beginning to relax when my grandmother said, "Honey, I'm worried about you. You've gained weight since you started that church job, and I just don't know how you're ever going to get a husband if you insist on working in a church and don't keep up your appearance. Maybe you should start that Weight Watcher's thing your cousin is doing or get a retail job with clothing discounts." Thanks, Grandma.

As young women, we have to respect ourselves and make changes to our bodies based on health reasons and not simply aesthetic motivations. If we feel we are too thin or too heavy, we should take a look at our daily routines and see what is unhealthy: too many lunches at our desks? fast food on the way home from church meetings? not sleeping enough? not taking time to exercise? Any number of stressors can make us feel unbalanced or unhappy with our bodies, and no attire or accessories can change how we feel internally.

All of this is compounded even further when we take into account that we, as young clergy women, are role models to other females. Teenage girls in our congregations look up to us and will see both the positive and negative ways we balance work, dating, family, and the rest of our lives. They will see us as examples of females dressing professionally or unprofessionally, criticizing or honoring ourselves, accepting a compliment when it is appropriate, and rejecting unwanted sexual advances when the compliment goes too far. They will notice the length of our skirts and if we always have cleavage in our low cut shirts.

And most importantly, they will notice how we talk about our bodies and other people's bodies.

Young clergy women must demonstrate that our value and our worth come from being called children of God and not from Gucci, *Cosmo*, or "Gossip Girl." We should portray a healthy lifestyle that nurtures our bodies and this life God has given us. God's claim on our lives gives us meaning and purpose regardless of our bra size, jean size, or bank account. God calls us to celebrate our bodies, our femininity, and ourselves. While figuring out how to dress like a young clergy woman is fraught with challenge, it can also be an opportunity to preach, teach, and heal our congregations and ourselves.

Wearing Purple without Apologies

Proverbs 31 offers us a royal perspective on the woman at work and particularly on her clothes. This text describes a capable wife or woman who has responsibilities both inside and outside the home. This virtuous woman obtains food, buys property, gives charity to the poor, loves her children, honors her home, and uses her industry to provide for her family. She laughs, she speaks, she charms, and she comforts. And according to the proverb, she has beautiful clothes. Perhaps as a reward to herself, she "makes herself coverings; her clothing is fine linen and purple" (Prov. 31:22). Proverbs is quick to remind us that a woman's fine wardrobe is not a sign of virtue; that is, people who dress well are not somehow more blessed by God. However, Proverbs does assure us that clothing can be an honor and a blessing when we use it as a celebration of our work and ourselves. It is not a sin to clothe ourselves in fine things as long as we remember that these fine things do not make us holy or blessed. Our attitude, our kindness, our commitment, and our faith guide our ministry. As Proverbs explains, when we abide in our faith, we are to be celebrated: "Charm is deceitful, and beauty is vain, but a woman who fears the Lord is to be praised. Give her a share in the fruit of her hands, and let her works praise her in the city gates" (Prov. 31:30–31).

For ministers, a "share in the fruit of our hands" may be that we risk wearing whatever clothing we deem appropriate. When we work hard, we should feel free to reward ourselves, which may mean wearing whatever clerical garb makes us comfortable in our ministry. Perhaps we spend too much on our dream Cole Haans with Nike Air insoles that we *know* belong on our feet. Perhaps we wear jeans when appropriate, put our hair up when we need it out of the way, and highlight it when we get the urge. If we like our legs and feel confident in how that skirt looks, then we should wear it boldly and often. We may continue to get those annoying comments about our dress, but when we find an article of clothing that celebrates our body, honors our labor, and complements our virtue, we should feel free and happy to wear it with style.

Presenting Our Bodies

We also have to remember that honoring our bodies is a social issue as well as a personal one. We may be called to present ourselves in ways we might not choose were we in another profession, and to make sacrifices for the good of the community. Despite our frustrations, we are looked on by our congregation as a model—both for how to dress and how to behave. This can be daunting, and sometimes our role as a model can stray too far. Yet we serve as models, especially for the young women of our congregation who are confronted daily with negative stereotypes about their bodies. With these young women in mind, we realize that how we present our bodies—how we dress—is vital to maintaining and building the community of faith. We can wear the favorite skirt with sass, but we should also have the wisdom and judgment to recognize when the skirt is really wearing us.

Paul's metaphor of the church as the body of Christ means that each of us is called with different gifts into Christ's service. The body needs every person and every gift: "For just as the body is one and has many members, and all the members of the body, though many, are one body, so it is with Christ" (1 Cor. 12:12). Because of our connection within the body of Christ, God calls us to honor our gifts, our ministries, and our bodies in a way that builds up the entire body, not only our own part. When Paul discusses the body of Christ in Romans, he says,

> I appeal to you therefore, brothers and sisters, by the mercies of God, to present your bodies as a living sacrifice, holy and acceptable to God, which is your spiritual worship. Do not be conformed to this world, but be transformed by the renewing of your minds, so that you may discern what is the will of God—what is good and acceptable and perfect. (Rom. 12:1–2)

Paul is not calling us to *be* perfect but to present ourselves with perfect intention. In order to be the body of Christ, we have to belong to each other. We are connected in meaningful, tangible, and even physical ways, the same way that the hand is connected to the foot, to the brain, and to the heart.

When we present our bodies as a living sacrifice, we must remember that we may sacrifice for the good of our body and the body of Christ. This may mean investing in those pinstripe suits that bore us to death but are vital to the role we serve in our community. It may mean covering up a little more, even when we can pull it off, so that both women and men can focus on our words and actions rather than our bodies. Finding the balance between celebrating our femininity and serving our community can be a delicate task. Yet since we are connected to others in a physical way, we acknowledge that being a pastor means thinking, feeling, believing, and dressing the part.

Being the Body

When it comes to dress, we have to strike a balance between celebrating our bodies and taking responsibility for the role our bodies play in the body of Christ. On one hand, we should seek out those beautiful adornments that enhance our physical, spiritual, and emotional lives. Just as the whole of the body is impacted by the one who suffers, so too is our whole body affected when we think negatively about that one part that drives us crazy. Every part of our bodies is to be honored and cherished: our legs, hips, smiles, breasts, feet, and everything else—even our butts and thighs, or our "aunties" as Anne Lamott calls them.[1] All these parts are gifts created by God and something we should be thankful for. Yet we are called to respond in ways that honor the entirety of these gifts. We are to live with a courageous spirit, loving ourselves in every possible way, both individually and as a member and a leader in the community. With that spirit of balance in mind, we offer the following memorable and constructive lessons shared by several grateful clergy women.

Top Ten Lessons about Being the "Body" of Christ

10. "I once had a colleague who had to tell me straight out that my shirts were too low cut. She was right, and I was glad that she just told me how it was, rather than talking behind my back. And, really, I think she was more embarrassed about our conversation than I was."

9. "I used to get nervous about my shoes, until one of the older ladies in my church said she loved my red shoes on Pentecost. Not nervous anymore!"

8. "Today a gentleman from my congregation told me that I looked beautiful, and I am always happy to take that compliment."

7. "Sometimes we forget how great it is to be a woman in the church. Once a young girl from the congregation ran up to me after the service and said, with this huge grin, 'I didn't know girls could do that!' That just made my day."

6. "I had a mentor and colleague tell me that I didn't need to stop wearing my scarves and 'dangly' earrings simply because I had received a few negative comments. She said there is nothing wrong with having my own flair with my black suit and that 'unique' and 'professional' aren't contradicting terms."

5. "The committee meeting was in a scalding hot room. I took off my suit jacket to cool off, but then my colleague said, 'Why don't you put that back on?' In the moment, I was angry. But she was right—I was much more comfortable when I felt professional than when I felt hot."

4. "I took notes during staff meetings on my iPhone until a female colleague told me that she overheard the other pastors talking about how disrespectful it was that the 'new young lady always texts during meetings.' My initial response was something rude about older generations until she said, 'You can continue to take notes on your phone, but just remember that you have to choose your battles, and you're the first young female pastor on this staff.' With those words of wisdom, I started taking notes the old fashioned way with pen and paper. And it was worth it."

3. "I realized I had put on a lot of weight in seminary, so in my first call, I brought lunch from home and spent the time working out. I was concerned that my colleagues would criticize me for not going out to lunch with them. But when I had lost a few pounds, they said I looked beautiful and they were proud of me. So was I."

2. "People always say to me, 'We love when you lead worship. We can always hear you and you speak so clearly and with confidence and the simple, easy response that we always love to hear.'"

1. "You're a pastor? Cool."

5

Pregnant in the Pulpit

Pregnancy and Maternity Leave

It is said that the present is pregnant with the future.

—Voltaire

We have established that leading worship can be a bit uncomfortable for clergy: the robes, the lights, the eyes staring back at you. Being a pregnant pastor amplifies this situation even further. No amount of book learning or imparted wisdom can fully prepare any woman for her first pregnancy, and women in ministry have the added adventure of learning about pregnancy with an anxious, excited, and perhaps *very* involved congregation. While we acknowledge that not every young clergy woman desires to or feels called to bear children, our congregations will probably still ask about our procreation plans regardless of our relationship status, health, or desire to enter into that discussion.

Women who are trying to conceive may be asked a number of questions about the timeline of medications and procedures, just as women who do not have children will likely be asked, "When?" or "Why not?" For some, not having children is a conscious choice. For others, it is a painful reality due to health complications or other factors. Regardless of where we personally come down on the desire to have children, we know that being pregnant and being a parent can be a wonderfully beautiful and new adventure. The pregnant and the not-so-pregnant pastor can find themselves in situations and conversations we probably did not learn about in seminary. As one pastor states,

> I get asked all the time when I am going to have kids while I am greeting church members at the end of the worship services. I don't believe for a second that they would be so interested in my procreation plans if I were an accountant filing their taxes.

While the pregnant pastor may endure a long list of questions, all young clergy women face a plethora of options and questions. And for all of us, this exhaustive list of life questions will have to be answered in some form and at some time in our ministry.

Getting the Question

I finally got an interview with the church I had hoped for. It was the right size and location, and the first interview over the phone had gone really well. This was to be my first call to a church, and my partner and I were ready to start a family and grow together in this loving and nurturing congregation. I could not believe it when, after the interview, I found out that I was pregnant. We had been praying for a baby, and the thought of a new baby and a new church was both daunting and exciting. We began to make tentative plans about houses, schools, and cribs. We told our closest friends and prayed daily for the health and strength of the baby growing inside of me.

After several months of waiting, I finally made it to church for an interview with the committee. When I walked into the room, I knew that they were surprised to see that I was visibly pregnant. But I felt like I handled their surprise with grace. We talked all about my visions for the church, my role as a pastor, and how I felt God calling and working in my life and in the life of the congregation. Even with their initial surprise, they seemed pleased and excited, and I felt like I was finally getting a chance to do the ministry I had felt called to my whole life.

As the interview closed, I found myself laughing and joking with the committee members but was already starting to ask myself the internal questions of church growth and childcare. Suddenly a much different question came from out of nowhere: "Tell me: what is the point of being a pastor if you are already pregnant?" I snapped back to attention and locked eyes with the elderly gentleman who had been quiet for most of the interview. It took a moment for the question to sink in, but then it hit me: This person thought that I had the option to either be a pastor or be a mom. For him, it was one or the other. My ministry was just a stopover between childhood and motherhood. I swallowed hard and stumbled through some kind of answer about vocation and calling, but I could feel both the heat coming out of my ears and the tears welling up in my eyes.

What made me the angriest, however, was that lingering suspicion that he might be right. Was I going to be ready to leave my baby in the church daycare every day while I ran to and from visiting members in the hospital? Was I going to be able to be both a good pastor and a good mom? Was I going to be able to find a place that honored the challenges of pregnancy, the gifts of children, and the future I had in store? And could I do it all when the time came? Did anyone ever ask a man whether he could be a dad and a pastor at the same time?

> I left the interview deflated and angry with dozens
> of questions circling my head. I went home, collapsed on
> the bed, and told my partner that I just wasn't sure what
> to do next.

Often the personal boundaries found in most professions are simply not the same for pastors. Many congregations recognize this and try to ensure that they respect the pastor's privacy. Some personnel committees, especially those whose members have backgrounds in human resources or the legal profession, work to ensure female clergy are not asked inappropriate in an interview or annual review. One second-career pastor states,

> I was visibly pregnant when I was given a huge promotion, and the topic was never discussed. I signed the papers for the promotion, received a great pay increase, and took my maternity leave per regulations of the Family and Medical Leave Act. Then again, I had worked as an attorney for a large firm, so I suppose they knew better.

Yet in some cases, pastors are expected to devote not just their profession but their *lives* to the ministry. Congregations, particularly small ones without a large staff, may have legitimate concerns about how they will handle a pastor on maternity leave. Young clergy women are sometimes asked to walk the fine line between honest concern and illegal questions. Some may choose to be open about their procreation plans, and others may opt to keep that information private.

Sometimes it can be difficult for a congregation to understand that even if you are partnered or married, you may not be ready to have children or feel called to be parents. Often congregation members inquire about our pregnancy plans or pregnancy because they love us and would love to see us in the role of parents. This is not a bad thing; on the contrary, it can be flattering. In the same way, not all inquiries come from a place of being nosey, but come from a desire for connection and pastoral care. For instance, when the sixty-year-old woman asks you if you are trying to have children, she may be looking for a way to tell you that her daughter-in-law is newly pregnant. In the same way, when the thirty-five-year-old man asks your husband if you are thinking of having kids, he may be more interested in talking through his own challenges with adoption than prying into your life. Yet because of the difference in boundaries, and the delicacy of being pregnant and bearing children, these attempts at dialogue can seem out of place or inappropriate, and take a young clergy woman off guard.

While the driving force behind the litany of questions may be respect for us or the desire to talk to us about this intimate subject, the questions themselves can become exhausting and painful. If you have had a miscarriage or are having trouble conceiving, these questions can make you feel as if you've been hit in the gut. Many pastors who have trouble conceiving or have recently lost a child testify to how difficult is it when they are asked, "When are you going to start a family?" This is a perfectly innocent question, perhaps one that you may have wondered about or asked of friends and colleagues. Our inclination may be to shout, "None of your business!" but the pastoral response will hopefully sound different, or at least more polite. One clergy woman responds this way:

> When I get asked when I'm going to have kids, I just smile and say, "You know, with the twenty teenagers I'm in charge of, that's about all the family I can handle right now." There's not much anybody can say to that.

In addition to the potentially painful or seemingly nosey questions, many clergy women find that officiating the sacrament of baptism can also be very difficult at times. One clergy woman recalls the following:

> I had a miscarriage early in my pregnancy and only told close friends and family. I had great therapy sessions and helpful discussions with my physician, and felt good about where I was in my grief process—until

I was asked to do a baptism. I had officiated many baptisms prior to my own loss and have always loved what baptism represents, but suddenly I was nauseated at the thought of it. What if I cried through the whole thing? What if I was jealous of that couple's healthy baby? I called my therapist for an emergency session but still didn't sleep that Saturday night before the baptism. I prayed for courage and strength, and asked God if I was fit to be a parent. As I drove to church that Sunday, I began to feel a peace deep within my gut that indeed surpassed all human understanding. Then, as I held that healthy baby in my arms, dipped my hand in the waters of grace, and proclaimed, "You are a child of the covenant," I was overcome with gratitude. Not gratitude for my loss but gratitude for the opportunity to hold a healthy baby as a tangible reminder that the covenant continues. Maybe I will be a biological mother and maybe I won't, but I am still a child of the covenant. And as a pastor, I have the great privilege of proclaiming that others are, too.

If and when you do conceive a child, then how do you tell your congregation you're pregnant? According to many young clergy women, this is one of the toughest questions we can face in our ministry. Many women find themselves anxious, frightened, and emotional at the very thought of the big moment. One pastor said,

When I had to tell my colleague I was pregnant, I was a nervous wreck. Really, that was the one of the hardest parts of my first few months of pregnancy—not morning sickness, not financial pressures, but simply telling the other pastor what was about to happen. With all our responsibilities and schedules, with just a few of us on staff and a whole congregation to attend to, how would he respond to the fact that I would be out of commission *for months*?

In a situation like this one, it becomes important to know the culture of your congregation and anticipate how people across the board will respond. Do you begin with the senior pastor, the bishop, or the personnel committee? Do you break the news first to your friends in ministry and then move on to the women's Bible study?

Just as the woman in our story was not able to predict how the committee would respond, we may be surprised by either the support or neglect we receive from our congregations. While certain people and situations can be frustrating, the experiences of raising a child in a community of faith can have unexpected rewards. As one new mother said,

> I won't pretend those first few months were easy. I was so exhausted a lot of the time and still trying to figure out what kind of mommy I was. The congregation tried to be helpful, but few of them were young parents, and there were so many times when I just wanted to scream and quit and punch something. But during that time, I learned so much about what I was capable of, what I needed to do myself and what I could let go of, and what being a mom, a wife, and a minister meant for me. Eventually, I was able to be clear and honest about what I could do. This experience led me to a new ministry with an understanding church staff and congregation. I am blessed to raise my child in a supportive community and now I am better able to balance work and my family, enjoying the both of them so much more.

Contemplating all the blessings, questions, and options might make your brain hurt, but they are the very issues every female pastor is challenged to consider as she is navigating the waters of pregnancy and children. Not all of us will face all of these questions, but the beauty and frustration of our ministries may mean that we have many more options and questions than we could have imagined. The questions that face the pregnant pastor are often a microcosm of the questions that await all of us. But when charged with answering these questions, knowing that we are not alone is a comforting first step.

A Dubious List

There is no lack of scriptural precedence in the pregnancy department: Sarah, the mother of Isaac; Hagar, the mother of Ishmael; Hannah, the mother of Samuel; Rebekah, the mother of Esau and Jacob; Rachel, the mother of Benjamin and Joseph; Naomi, the mother-in-law of Ruth; and so on. All of these women are honored in scripture for their contributions and, perhaps most of all, for their pregnancies. Some had difficulties conceiving, some had children who died, and some even became pregnant against their will. Yet it is clear that God cherishes pregnancy.

This is especially evident in the genealogy of Jesus. In this first chapter, the gospel of Matthew lists the generations that came before the birth of the Messiah. For all the men listed whose names we have almost forgotten—Abiud, Salathiel, Matthan—there are only a handful of women mentioned on this list. Those women are Tamar, Rahab, Ruth, the wife of Uriah (Bathsheba), and Mary. Given the number of scriptural matriarchs whose children are included on this genealogical list, this is a strange group of ladies to mention. Tamar has two husbands killed for their wickedness and then is almost burned to death. Rahab is a prostitute who betrays her city for favor with the Israelites. Ruth is a widow from outside the community, David steals Bathsheba through murder (and she doesn't even get mentioned by name in the genealogy), and Mary finds herself in the "trinitarian" situation of young, unmarried, and pregnant.

Why would Matthew want to include these particular women? Perhaps Matthew wants to remind us that God can use traumatic and unjust situations for good. Even from these troubled unions, and the pain and misery of these five women, Jesus is born. Moreover, he is born to be a messiah for just these kinds of women: the widows, the prostitutes, and the outsiders.

We can recite these names in Jesus' genealogy when we are frustrated by the realities of being pregnant in the pulpit.

We may have difficult pregnancies: There are the "Sarahs" of the world, who may be too old to have a child; there are the "Hannahs," who wait many years to get pregnant; and there are "Rebekahs," who struggle with the relationships between their children. There are even the "Michals" who, like David's wife, are unable to sustain a pregnancy and end up parenting other people's children. And yet as pastors, our pregnancies can be a step beyond. We can easily feel like the "Tamars," whose families are judged, or the "Ruths," who are foreign outsiders to the mainstream. Remembering that we are daughters of these women can help us fulfill the roles of mother and pastor. In our life and ministry, we too are listed within the genealogy of Jesus and are called to be God's messengers. The women of our ancestry strengthen our faith, and their stories give us courage as we see motherhood portrayed in many forms. And we find great hope in the promise that we are all heirs of God's covenant.

Jumping for Joy

One of the most powerful announcements of pregnancy is between the cousins Mary and Elizabeth. Mary is pregnant with Jesus and has already endured the social stress of being pregnant out of wedlock while engaged to Joseph. To add to the shock and awe, the angel proclaimed to Mary that her cousin Elizabeth was also pregnant with a son. This pregnancy, too, was miraculous as Elizabeth was said to be too old to conceive. The angel declared to Mary, "And now, your relative Elizabeth in her old age has also conceived a son; and this is the sixth month for her who was said to be barren. For nothing will be impossible with God." Mary responded, "Here am I, the servant of the Lord; let it be with me according to your word" (Lk. 1:36–38).

In this amazing and exhausting first trimester, Mary journeys to Judea to visit Elizabeth. As soon as Elizabeth hears Mary's voice, the baby in Elizabeth's womb leaps for joy, and

Elizabeth is filled with the Spirit of God. Elizabeth joyfully greets Mary proclaiming,

> Blessed are you among women, and blessed is the fruit of your womb. And why has this happened to me, that the mother of my Lord comes to me? For as soon as I heard the sound of your greeting, the child in my womb leaped for joy. And blessed is she who believed that there would be a fulfillment of what was spoken to her by the Lord. (Lk. 1:42–45)

Every announcement of pregnancy is not so exuberantly documented. But for those who are trying to conceive a child, the miracle of new life and the overflowing joy is just as miraculous as it was for Mary and Elizabeth. Each pregnancy has its share of social stresses and family stresses, morning sickness, body changes, and schedule changes. Yet pregnancy is a tangible sign that God is constantly creating and recreating. The capacity to be such an integral part of God's plan for the world is an amazing gift. God speaks through pregnant women, both inside and outside of the pulpit. When we are blessed with the opportunity to speak God's word through our bodies, our response may be the same as Mary's: "Here I am, the servant of the Lord; let it be with me according to your word" (Lk. 1:38).

It Takes a Village

The questions and lessons that face the pregnant pastor can be difficult and hard won. In the midst of anticipating a beautiful new life, we may grow frustrated by both our hormonal bodies and the inevitable challenges that surround our work as clergy. However, it is sanity saving to remember the gifts of joy and laughter as we approach announcing our pregnancy, hanging curtains in our office for breast-feeding, or making sure the Pack 'n Play will fit in the church van. Through humor and excitement, our frustrations are transformed into opportunities, and we find unexpected reasons to celebrate. And on the days we feel overwhelmed by people in our business, it is humbling to remember that those same people brought meals for weeks after the birth of our child, made baptismal promises on his or her behalf, and are sincere in their offers to baby-sit. There is a reason they say that it "takes a village" to raise children. Thankfully, as clergy women serving congregations, we have a village full of grandparents, aunts, and uncles for our children even if our biological families are a few states away.

I was sixth months' pregnant with my fourth child when I started having major complications, and my health and the baby's were in jeopardy. The day I realized something was very wrong, I called my neighbor and asked her to watch my three children after school while I went to an emergency doctor's appointment. After a series of tests, he came back in the room with a look of panic and said softly, "Call your husband and have him meet you at the hospital. I'm admitting you for observation."

The next few hours were a blur, but I remember frantically calling neighbors, colleagues, and my husband, who was out of town. Once I was settled in my hospital room and hooked up to various monitors and cords, I curled up on my side and wept. My cell phone battery was dead. I couldn't reach my husband. I couldn't hug my children. I had no idea what would happen to my unborn baby or me. I was terrified, absolutely terrified.

An hour after I was admitted, a colleague arrived with my favorite foods and my three children in tow. As my children climbed all over my bed they chattered about their day and asked tons of questions about the hospital. When there was a brief lull amid the chatter, my colleague said, "I've gotten in touch with your husband, and he's at the airport trying to change his flight. My wife and I are going to stay at your house tonight with the kids. Tomorrow, Susan from your Bible study will take them to school, and Margie from your VBS committee will pick them up. If your husband is not back by then, my wife and I will spend tomorrow night, too." As everything he said began to sink in, I started crying again. I was so overwhelmed with gratitude that I couldn't even speak.

I hugged and kissed our children good-night about the time my husband called the hospital to say he was on the first flight out in the morning. As I was hanging up the phone, a church member appeared with flowers, movies, a phone charger, and an overnight bag. Ignoring the shock on my face she smiled, "I figure you won't be getting much sleep tonight and might like some company." While I attempted to object, she put the flowers in a vase, her pillow in the chair, and turned on the DVD player. She gently took my hand and said, "You can pretend you're fine all you want, but you are crazy if you think any of us are going to leave you here alone tonight. You sit back and use that energy to get you and that baby well."

I am thrilled to report that my newborn baby and I are healthy. I am also humbled to share how our neighbors and church family cared for us. They took "it takes a village" and "love your neighbor" to new levels, and we literally couldn't have survived without them. You know, it's funny, I remember telling my husband after my interview, "I'd love the opportunity to love and serve this group of people if this is where we are supposed to be." Clearly we are where we are supposed to be, and they love us in ways we could have never imagined.

6

Jesus Wept

The Role and Power of Emotions

*The emotions aren't always immediately subject
to reason, but they are always immediately subject
to action.*

—WILLIAM JAMES

How many times have you heard someone say—or, if they
didn't say it, you know they thought to themselves—that you
were just letting your emotions get to you? As young women
we bring our sadness, anger, joy, and fear to our ministry.
Some might tell you to set aside these emotions for the sake of
professionalism, but they are tools and gifts for our ministry.
Our emotions are part of being fearfully and wonderfully made
(Ps. 139:14). God gives them to us as powerful gifts, and with
them we can honor God and build up communities of faith.
But like all gifts, we have to use them in the right situations

and for the right purposes. As young clergy women, harnessing our emotive power can create opportunities for ministry, even when the emotions themselves don't come out exactly as we planned.

These Damn Flowers

Let's be honest: I didn't mean to scream out, "Come get these damn flowers!" to the elderly parishioner on the phone. It just happened. Most unfortunately, it happened on Easter Sunday.

I was completely exhausted. I had led a service every day for the last eight days. My parents were in town and were getting annoyed that I couldn't find one hour to come have some Easter dinner with them. And I was up to my eyeballs in lilies that had to be delivered to nursing homes across town before I could go home and collapse. The system for figuring out who had signed up to take flowers and where they were going had completely fallen apart, and so it fell to me alone to figure out how to deliver fifty lilies to elderly folks on Easter. Although I took some refuge in the risen Christ on that particular day, I also forgot all about Him when I realized that my volunteer lily organizer was unable to come by and help me sort out the mess. She had promised, insisted, assured me that her delivery system would work, and when it didn't, she had disappeared, leaving me in a pile of pollen. So here it was: pushing 3:00 p.m. on Easter Sunday, and I was screaming at her over the phone.

Apparently, I was also screaming in front of the choir. Yes, the entire choir, all of whom had stayed after the service for a lunch hosted by the music director. En masse, they came around the corner to see me yelling at the top of my lungs, unable to control my volume any longer. This got me more than just some stern glares. I also got several phone calls, a lecture from the music director, a talking-to from the bishop—and the opportunity to grovel in front of the poor woman I yelled at.

I never meant to get that angry over something as silly as lilies, and certainly not on Easter. But in that moment, I simply was incapable of holding it in any longer. My voice could not be quiet. I was tired and wanted a chance to celebrate Easter with my family, and I just had to yell as loud as I could and hope that someone out there heard me. Sadly, lots of people did.

Newspapers are full of stories about pastors who hit the wall and found some inappropriate way to express their emotions. At the times when we are most vulnerable and exhausted from lack of structure, crazy schedules, sermon writing, long hours of pastoral care, and life itself, it is understandable that our emotional stability is not at its best. Just the schedules of Lent or Advent alone are enough to leave clergy fatigued and in a valley of dry bones. However, if there are any additional stressors in your life—funerals, weddings, or drama in your family—you can go from barely holding it together to breaking point in no time.

Moreover, as women, we also face the judgment and anxiety that goes along with tears and rage. With the looming stereotype of the magnanimous, self-sufficient pastor, it's not enough for us to keep our emotions in check; even generally appropriate ways of expressing ourselves cross the line for some, especially with the always-present stereotypes of the hysterical woman. It may be a completely suitable response to cry, scream, or jump with joy, but showing any of these emotions may invite criticism from both men and women. Yet as young women in ministry, we can find ourselves in stressful or even dangerous situations. Particularly in these instances, our emotions are sources for health, wellness, growth, and learning. They can let us know when something is going right or wrong:

I was attempting to visit a dying parishioner in the hospital when I entered through the wrong door. I found myself in a closed-down wing of the hospital, completely abandoned and creepy. I was nervous and almost jumped out of my skin when a large man came around the corner and spotted me. He began walking quickly toward me, and I hauled my butt down the hallway, out the door, and back to the church. I felt stupid for freaking out the way I did and felt horrible for leaving the hospital without visiting the congregant. But a pastor at the church reassured me: "You did the right thing," he said. "Always trust your instincts. Sometimes that feeling in your gut is your best friend in ministry."

Our emotions are a part of God's creation, just like our bodies, souls, and minds. Recognizing the power of our emotions can make us feel vulnerable, but they can also open us up to real opportunities for ministry—to ourselves and to our congregations.

As pastors, we face unexpected, complicated, and highly emotional issues daily. We also have lives outside of the church that bring their own stressors and can affect our emotional state at work. Amid the challenges of ministry, both inside and outside the church, it is only a matter of time before our own emotions take hold. In the example of "These Damn Flowers," yelling over the phone was clearly not the most appropriate way to express frustration over the logistics and details of Easter. But it doesn't make this pastor any less of a pastor. In this case, the young clergy woman survived her first Easter—not without mistakes or embarrassment—but also accepted the criticism, apologized, and learned from her mistakes.

When it comes to the explosive power of emotions, expression and forgiveness are the name of the game. We will all, at some point, hit the emotional wall. Some of us will respond out loud, and some of us will hold it all in. In either case, we have to find appropriate ways to express and contain our emotions for the sake of our work. When we do that poorly—and we will—we have to be willing to forgive ourselves and move on. As Henri Nouwen stated, "Forgiveness is the name of love practiced among people who love poorly."[1] When called into the extravagant love of ordained ministry, our callings will often be emotionally difficult, and we must remain willing to ask for and receive forgiveness when we find ourselves in the wrong.

To maintain the balance between appropriate expression and unhelpful stoicism, it is essential that we keep ourselves in check and have others who hold us accountable for our emotional and spiritual life. We need others who can tell us to regroup, calm down, or even shut up before saying something we will regret or doing something we would never do otherwise. No pastor is an island, and no one is able to maintain a critical eye on his or her emotions without the support of others. For many of us, colleagues in ministry are few and far between. We must intentionally seek out people we can talk to confidentially about the joys and concerns of our jobs and work to maintain those friendships even as our time and energy is stretched.

Finally, as clergy we have to remember that our emotions are an essential aspect of our daily work. We are blessed with the unique privilege and responsibility of meeting others in the midst of their greatest joy, suffering, and anger. Often, our first response is that we want to fix the emotions, take the pain away, and make everything all right. Or we are so fully aware that we cannot fix everything that we become exhausted from being just as vulnerable as the person to whom we are offering care and support. As hard as it is to wonder why bad things happen to good people, and as draining as it is to be fully present with others in their deep valleys, we must remember that there is no greater honor than being invited into the lives of others. There are few situations as intimate and holy as being allowed to be with a family as their matriarch takes her last breath or being in the waiting room with parents when they receive the good news of their child's surgery. As "wounded healers,"[2] we can treasure these moments of holy ground by allowing our emotions and gut feelings to guide us rather than inhibit us.

How Long, O Lord?

The songs, poems, and laments of the Psalms offer opportunities to pray in the midst of just about every conceivable human emotion. Psalm 23 speaks to us in grief; Psalm 150 celebrates elation; Psalm 55 speaks to us when we are frightened; and Psalm 73 can give words to our anger. No emotion has been ruled out as inappropriate or unfitting. Rather, the Psalms can give words and prayers to emotions we might never acknowledge to others or within ourselves—violent thoughts, illogical jealousy, consuming envy, irrational joy, or debilitating depression.

The Psalms are also a source of great comfort to clergy as we are reminded over and over again that we are not alone in our laments or our joys. We, too, need to be reminded of the many who have gone before us whose voices echo throughout the Psalms. Perhaps most important, we need the reminder that the Psalms, like all scripture, while inspired by God, are written by finite and sinful humans, just like us. We seek refuge in the Psalms and are nourished by the Psalms because we, too, are beautifully human.

One woman tells of her reliance on the Psalms in her ministry:

> I work at a shelter for women and children, most of whom are victims of domestic abuse and violence. When I meet them, many feel hopeless, defeated, and weary, and wonder if the pain will ever go away. One woman said, "God must have forgotten me, because He never stopped my husband from hitting me. If I hadn't run away, it would have gone on forever." During my initial meeting with these women, I listen to their stories, then read this psalm aloud to them:
>
> > How long, O Lord? Will you forget me forever? How long will you hide your face from me? How long must I bear pain in my soul, and have sorrow in my heart all day long?

How long shall my enemy be exalted over me? Consider and answer me, O Lord my God! Give light to my eyes, or I will sleep the sleep of death, and my enemy will say, 'I have prevailed;' my foes will rejoice because I am shaken. But I trusted in your steadfast love; my heart shall rejoice in your salvation. I will sing to the Lord, because he has dealt bountifully with me. (Ps. 13)

When I ask them what they hear in the psalm, their responses include, "that I'm not the only one God forgot," or "I am not alone," or "Now that I'm gone, I have an answer to how long the beatings will last." After they describe what they heard, I ask them to read it aloud to me. I have yet to encounter a woman for whom this is not a powerful experience, and I am grateful to have such a powerful Scripture to share with them. God's healing power is expressed through the shared lament, and for these women, hope springs forth from wounds that will heal.

Jesus Cries Out

Throughout Christ's ministry there are glimpses of his fully human emotions that are powerful and comforting. We see his anger at the money changers in the temple, his joy around children, his frustration with the Pharisees and Sadducees, his compassion for the sick, and his tears and grief for his friend Lazarus. His grief over Lazarus' death is perhaps one of the times when Jesus is most vulnerable. The Jews in nearby Jerusalem were plotting against him, yet he goes to Bethany after Lazarus has been dead for four days. He is filled with such empathy as Mary and Martha weep and cry out for their brother that he also cries and joins them in their pain. Jesus tries to explain to them that death no longer has the final say, but that does not take away their sadness and longing for their brother. Through his own tears, Jesus goes to Lazarus' tomb and loudly cries, "Lazarus, come out!" To everyone's shock, Lazarus does come out with his feet, hands, and face still bound with strips of cloth. Jesus said to those standing by, "Unbind him, and let him go" (Jn. 11:43–44).

This scene does not seem like just another miracle healing. Rather, it seems that Jesus commanding Lazarus to come out is rooted in empathy for human pain and his knowledge that death does not have the final world. This is Jesus making a bold statement to "come out!" and face life instead of death. We can imagine it spoken through tears and the choppy breathing of someone grieving. It is true that Jesus pleads for Lazarus to be unbound not only so that the grief of the community is eased. But he, himself, is also in grief. He pleads for Lazarus to come out of despair and experience hope that is alive. Through his own tears, Jesus loudly cried out to the tomb. His own emotions are a part of the miracle.

As pastors we proclaim in word and in deed that death no longer has the final say and has been defeated by the risen Christ. We understand that "the Word became flesh and dwelt among us" (Jn. 1:14) out of God's unconditional love for humanity. The God we serve is active in our world and continues to create, recreate, and restore our brokenness and pain. We know, every day, sometimes through our tears, that Jesus is standing at the tombs of our lives and our loved ones loudly crying, "Come out!" Following Jesus' example, we are not called to be emotionally separate from the anger and grief around us. Rather, when we tap into the power of our emotions, we can perform our own style of miracles by unbinding the brokenhearted and crying out the truth of life eternal in Christ.

I Don't Know

When Jesus' emotions influenced his ministry, he brought about one of his most powerful miracles. It may be frightening when our emotions influence our ministry, but when we allow our emotions to speak the truth, we find ourselves in opportunities for ministry that we could never have imagined. It is precisely in our most vulnerable moments that our own desires for control and eloquence are set aside. In these moments, the Spirit of God freely speaks through us and in spite of us.

I was the chaplain on duty during a thirty-hour shift when I received a call from the labor and delivery charge nurse at about 3:00 a.m. She said she needed me "as soon as you can get yourself here." I stumbled around the room to find my eye drops and a toothbrush and headed down to labor and delivery. When I checked in with the charge nurse she said, "This one will break your heart. She's twenty-five, been married two years, and is thirty weeks pregnant with triplets. Their whole family has been called and wants to be here when she delivers, so we are waiting for her parents, then we'll get going. She has only known for thirty minutes that two of the three babies have died, and the third may not make it through delivery. They asked for a chaplain to come pray for the third baby."

With that, I knocked on the door, entered, and saw a beautiful twenty-five-year-old woman sitting up in bed and weeping, her husband curled up in bed with her, and their siblings and his parents surrounding them. They asked me to pray for the third baby's lungs, heart, and chance at life, so I joined the cloud of witnesses around her hospital bed and began to pray. After holy moments of tears and silence, the young mother looked at me and asked if I would go tell the nurse she was ready to deliver.

The nurses and doctors were compassionate, visibly upset, and offered their condolences to the family. She delivered after only a short time and soon found out that the third baby had also died. In what seemed like slow motion, I witnessed their world crumble around them as they held their three babies. They caressed them and commented on their hair and fingers and toes as any new parents do and knew that they will never get haircuts or use their fingers and toes to run and play. One of the nurses grabbed my hand as she was shaking and crying; another nurse had to leave the room. The young mother asked me to pray with her, so we all joined hands again to talk to our Creator. I ended the prayer, as I always end prayers of infant death: "In the name of the One who welcomes all children home, Amen."

As I completed the chart at the nurses' station, the grandfather of those three babies came out of the room and asked to speak with me. I walked with him to an empty waiting area. We sat down, and he looked at me with tears streaming down his face and said, "I just assembled three cribs in their nursery and three changing tables, and now I have to take them apart. What do I do with those cribs apart when they are supposed to be filled with life and joy? How can I take them apart?" His eyes never left mine, and I as listened to him, I felt my eyes filling up with tears and soon felt them running down my face. We sat in that waiting room, eyes locked, crying, and all I could muster was "I don't know." He dropped his head in his hands and continued crying as I reached for tissues for both of us. He then stood up, said he wanted to tell his three grandchildren good-bye one last time, and went back to the room.

I spent the rest of that day feeling guilty for crying in front of him and inadequate for not saying something comforting or reassuring. As clergy we are trained to "game face" in crisis situations and have our own breakdowns later. We are intentional about "not making it about us" and being fully present with the families we are serving. I felt I had failed.

When I arrived at the main entrance to the hospital the next day, I saw the grandfather waiting for me. I greeted him and shook his hand. As I held his hand he said, "I just wanted to thank you for our conversation yesterday.

In my sixty-five years, I have never had a religious figure tell me it was OK to question God or admit they don't have all the answers. Your obvious grief and pain for my grandchildren and admitting that you don't know was exactly what I needed from someone representing my God. I just wanted you to know that."

In shock and awe, I gave thanks to God for those tears and prayed that I may never be ashamed to boldly proclaim, "I don't know."

7

Make Yourself at Home

Staying Grounded in Your New Call

*When I learn something new—and it happens
every day—I feel a little more at home in this
universe, a little more comfortable in the nest.*

—BILL MOYERS

Regardless of childhood or upbringing, each of us knows
what home was, is, or what we dream it will be. For some, home
is a tangible, four-walled place insulated with memories, and
for others home is a significant person, a city, or even a piece
of furniture or a picture. Some call home a specific smell, taste,
or feeling. Wherever, whomever, and whatever you call home,
home is where you go in a crisis, where you are loved, where
you are safe, and where you are accepted. Home is where you
are grounded during storms and where you are convinced you

are not alone in this world. At every age, sometimes we just need to go home.

The transition from graduate student to ordained pastor often involves relocation. This can include moving to a new city, state, or country and choosing your first apartment, condo, or house. If you serve a congregation that offers a parsonage or manse, this means moving into a predetermined space and creatively making it yours. For many young clergy—male and female—the first-call relocation is the first time we will live apart from friends or family, the first time we will have an office to decorate, or the first time we will create a home with our new spouse or baby. These are exciting rites of passage and an opportunity to build on the foundations of who we are, but they can also challenge us to redefine what home, tradition, and comfort mean to us.

Defining home is even more challenging when we move to a culture or community that is much different from the one we are used to. Suddenly our home is filled with strangers who think differently, have different backgrounds, and may even speak a different language. As pastors, part of our job is welcoming people into the community of Christ, so we may find ourselves welcoming people into a place we barely know. We have to quickly learn the customs, the etiquette, the expectations, and the resources. One pastor said,

> I moved to my first church about a month before a major special event, and they wanted me to get some publicity for it. They expected me to get camera crews and lead articles, and I didn't even know the channel for NBC.

Moving into a new community can be an ending and beginning, a fresh start and a solemn good-bye. Making a home for ourselves means we have to figure out how we define "home" and then create an environment of both the tangible and intangible that can welcome, protect, and nurture us.

Painting the Walls

Since high school, neither my husband nor I have lived in one place for more than a year. We met while traveling, and went to different seminaries across the country, so we constantly found ourselves moving back and forth between coasts. Because of that, I never felt like we lived anywhere. So when we moved to Central America to begin a new ministry, I thought that this would be our chance to really make a home together. I thought it would be an opportunity to paint the walls. In moving around so much, I had never even painted my own walls before, but the concept of painting the walls has always evoked a feeling of home for me. I thought that if we planned to be in one place long enough to paint the walls, then we really must be home.

It's now three years later. We've lived in three different places and we have never painted the walls. Our first house was too small, and we spent a year living in a house that we knew wasn't really "home." We went all out in our next house and picked paint colors for every room, but it was too far from the church and we broke our lease after four months. In our new house, we apprehensively decided once again to try to paint the walls. But the roof leaked, which caused the paint on the walls to bubble, so we had to wait until the rainy season was over to fix the roof, and then to fix the walls, before we could paint. We just got the roof fixed, but now there's the possibility that we might move into a house owned by the church, which would mean more space, less rent—and a church committee that will have to approve our decision to paint.

These are all the "house" reasons why we haven't painted the walls, but there are other reasons why it has been hard to call this place "home." I love this ministry, I love this country, and I have spent a lot of time in international ministries before, but serving here has proved to be very difficult. That sense of connectivity and "home" that I wanted has not really materialized the way I had hoped. My personal and professional life is conflated in ways that I never expected. It is almost impossible to meet people outside of the church. Even our casual acquaintances are somehow related to work, and sometimes I find myself in situations where my faith, my sense of justice, and my work are in conflict with each other. We still have to travel a lot and miss out on the weekend events that might make this place feel more like home. Even now, when I have finally started to find community with a group of women that I enjoy, few of them are my age, and my husband still hasn't found a group of friends outside of the church.

Our contracts are up soon, and we are back and forth about whether or not to stay. Some days my husband comes home and announces he's ready to leave, sometimes it's the other way around. I love my job, but I do think about moving closer to my family and friends. I honestly don't know where we will be a year from now or what our home will look like. All I know is regardless of where we go and which house we choose, we're painting the damn walls.

Without resorting to antiquated stereotypes, it does seem true that women like to make a nest. There is just something important, special, and uniquely feminine about creating a home. Even women with a partner and who may work long hours outside the home, still tend to shoulder most of the home responsibilities. Certainly, stay-at-home dads or opportunities for telecommunication mean that it can be easier for women to share the responsibilities of home with other members of the family. But homemaking is still something that women do, even *choose* to do, and often enjoy. Many of us love to search for just the right vase, cook up a mean pasta, or get the spare room ready for guests. This is not necessarily because as women we are supposed to do this; for many of us, it is part of how we practice hospitality.

But the realities of being hospitable, to others and ourselves, can make our transition into a new place challenging. When we move from seminary to call, young clergy women may be expected to create a home for themselves, to do it quickly, and perhaps most importantly, *cheaply*. Most of us will not rake in the cash in our first call, and so we have to take our futon, books, and odds and ends and figure out how to turn them into a nurturing environment. One young clergy woman, who moved five hundred miles away from her friends and family, did not have the money to move her furniture at all.

> I hit the IKEA and did the best I could. But after the thrill of the move and new adventure wore off, I found myself lonely in my very modern, yet very empty, loft. It didn't smell, feel, or look like my home. While I was visiting with my family over a holiday, I asked my grandmother if I could take a few pieces of home back with me. Now I have two hand-stitched blankets draped across my Karlstad sofa and some of her favorite candles in my bedroom. I so appreciate having these tangible reminders of home, and when I return from a long day of doing what I love, I think, "I *live* here. This is *my* home."

Creating a home can also mean that we have to create new ways of living in that home. Our home is of course much more than the physical space; it is the actions, occasions, and traditions that bring a house to life. Clergy of all ages and genders can be challenged by changes to the traditions of our lives, whether we are used to going out on a Saturday night with friends or spending holidays with our families. Our experiences of Christmas and Easter are fundamentally different from people in other professions, and it can be difficult for even the most well-intentioned family to grasp how we approach these seasons of the year. This may mean that we have to get creative with our holiday plans and figure out ways to turn a lonely house into a festive home:

The first time I had to spend Christmas Eve alone was the worst. I had put up all my old decorations and tried to make the cider my mom always made, but the decorations looked wilted in my little apartment, and the cider wasn't the same. So the next year, I knew I had to do something different. I splurged on a nice bottle of sake and made homemade sushi, complete with Christmas-colored salmon and avocado. It wasn't exactly home, but it wasn't sad either. Over the years, though, I sort of grew into it. Now my Christmas traditions include wrapping paper and rice paper.

Creating even the smallest new traditions for ourselves, from how we approach a quiet Saturday to how we prepare for major celebrations, can give us a steady point of ritual in the midst of a continually changing environment.

Making ourselves at home also requires that we get *out* of it. This is the challenge that leaves so many pastors feeling isolated and lonely. Without intentionality and persistence, it can be hard for even the most extroverted clergy woman to get out and make friends. Some of us find our social circle almost exclusively in the church, and some of us are less comfortable conflating "friends" with "congregants." Still, as the pastor stated in "Painting the Walls," it can be difficult to know where to meet people *if not* through the church. The pastor's schedule can mean there are few opportunities for social interaction. One pastor stated,

I had lived in this new town a year before I really made any friends. A woman from my church graciously invited me over to her house for a ladies night with several women from outside the church. I declined, because I was supposed to help with the youth retreat, but the sign-ups were low and the youth director canceled at the *very* last minute so I managed to meet up with the ladies. What a blessing! They were a riot and these women became a touchstone for me . . . and if the church hadn't canceled at the last minute, I would have missed it all.

Feeling at home in our home is important, but we are also called to feel at home—and we are to make others feel at home—in our church. People in other professions who relocate to other jobs or offices may feel the pressures to learn the language and get to know the natives, but the challenge to clergy is unique. Part of our calling is to welcome the stranger and shelter the afflicted. We rarely have the luxury of choosing who comes through the doors, and we pray that we never have to ask anyone to leave. Just as Jesus welcomed the children and ate with outcasts, pastors are expected to provide hospitality to all who come seeking refuge. When we are hospitable to ourselves—creating a nurturing home environment and welcoming the gifts and challenges of making ourselves at home—we are better equipped to live out our calling to welcome all pilgrims to the doors of our congregations. Whether it's beginning new traditions or painting the church walls, we can use our experiences in homemaking and home building to design and decorate a hospitable church.

Singing in Babylon

The Israelites were certainly no strangers to living abroad. The exile to Babylon is one of the most formative events recorded in the Hebrew scriptures with its implications spreading throughout the books of Jeremiah, Isaiah, Ezekiel, and many others. The words of Psalm 137 record the immense pain and suffering of a people uprooted from their home and brought into a wilderness society:

By the rivers of Babylon—there we sat down and there we wept when we remembered Zion. On the willows there we hung up our harps. For there our captors asked us for songs, and our tormentors asked for mirth, saying, "Sing us one of the songs of Zion!" How could we sing the Lord's song in a foreign land? (Ps. 137: 1–4)

Rather than being forced to sing for their captors, the displaced Israelites in this Psalm refuse to sing at all. They engage in lament and even envision a violent end to the Babylonians at the end of the verse, hanging up their harps and holding fast against the assimilation that Babylon encourages.

Hopefully, none of us feels this level of sorrow in our own calls. Yet we might identify with the feeling of living in a strange land where the songs of our past don't really fit in, where, as pastor Sam Martin says, "This language is not our language. This food is not our diet. The stories told to our children are not our stories. These values put on family and community are not our values."[1] We may already feel disconnected and unsure when we move into any new community, and churches have their own unique songs, narratives, and traditions that are not always easily understood. While we share the same Bible or hymnal, we don't know the songs, or histories, of our congregation. We have to learn whose mother died tragically and who is currently in recovery, along with the smaller, simpler aspects that make up the unique individuals and the congregation as a whole. Figuring out how to speak the language, who best to ask for advice, the intricacies of who handles the potluck and how communion is served are parts of the unique challenges of moving into a well-defined culture. Even in new church developments or new areas of ministry, we have to learn to tell the story of a community that may still be writing much of it. We may love this new land, but it can still be strange to us, and we are called to sing out our lives in the midst of a song that we simply don't know yet.

Learning to sing in a strange land can be metaphorical, but of course it can also be literal. Bringing in the songs of our past, the hymns and tunes that shaped us and nurtured us, can remind us that God's blessings are not limited to one place but travel along with us. A recent seminary graduate spoke about how each night, she turns off the television or Pandora and sings her favorite hymns—the praises and the laments—as she makes dinner. While she chops and stirs in the tiniest kitchen in New York City, this small act reminds her of her home in Virginia and brings the songs of her past into the beauty and frustrations of her present. While the Israelites could not sing in Babylon, we can and must sing out in the middle of what can be a strange land, and we can begin to learn the songs by singing ourselves, wherever and however we can.

Lessons of the Road

Our Christian faith calls us to radical acts of hospitality, and the example of Lydia in Acts shows us both how this is done and how we learn to do it. Paul and his entourage have traveled a long distance and arrive in Philippi. They are met by Lydia, who hears Paul's preaching, comes to believe in Christ, and offers the travelers hospitality. Acts says,

> A certain woman named Lydia, a worshiper of God, was listening to us; she was from the city of Thyatira and a dealer in purple cloth. The Lord opened her heart to listen eagerly to what was said by Paul. When she and her household were baptized, she urged us, saying, "If you have judged me to be faithful to the Lord, come and stay at my home." (Acts 16:14–15)

This offer of hospitality is a seemingly uncomplicated gesture. Paul needs a place to stay, and Lydia has a place—presumably, she has quite a big place since she is a garment merchant of some note—and as might be expected of a recent convert to Christianity, Lydia offers Paul's entourage her home.

But Lydia's offer of hospitality is rooted in more than a desire to serve. Lydia herself is a traveler. The text says she is from Thyatira, which is across the Aegean Sea from Macedonia. As biblical scholar Eric Barreto says,

> In a group of women listening to Paul and his companions, Lydia is highlighted . . . The naming of her hometown is an unexpected twist; despite the fact that a *Macedonian man* beckons the help of Paul, it is a *foreign*

woman who first has God open her heart to faith! . . .
For Lydia a natural result of her and her household's
receiving of the good news is to welcome these erst-
while strangers into her home.[2]

Lydia herself has experienced hospitality. The text indicates that
this foreign woman has been welcomed into Macedonia, and
as a powerful, wealthy woman, we can imagine that she would
have turned a few heads in this Roman city. Others have welcomed her, and in turn she is open to the Word and welcoming
to Paul. She is able to give hospitality because she has received
it, and she has received it as a result of being a traveler, of being
a pilgrim, of being open to the spiritual lessons of the road.

Our congregations are full of travelers who are seeking
God's call on their lives. Similarly, we may be seeking a welcoming community and learning how to navigate the challenges of
relocation and isolation. The example of Lydia shows us that
the ability to both offer and receive hospitality is intertwined.
When we challenge ourselves to truly welcome others, even
those who may not fit into our church home, we are better able
to seek out and receive that hospitality from the strangers in a
strange land.

A New York Bull in a Midwestern China Shop

Moving into a new environment can mean that we have
to create a new sense of home in the midst of a strange land.
For many pastors, the experience of being uprooted and
planted in a new place, perhaps very far away from friends or
colleagues, can breed a sense of isolation. Yet as pastors, we
are called to practice a unique form of hospitality, welcoming
others into a church home and creating a sense of community.
This strange challenge means that we must remember times
when we were welcomed and find ways to create a sense of
home for our congregations and ourselves. Moving into and
out of strikingly different communities can be difficult, but
when we are open to the workings of the Spirit, we may learn

the unexpected lessons of the pilgrim, traveling from home to home and back again.

I'm a native New Yorker. I was born and raised in the Bronx, and I lived my life between the Bronx and Harlem. When I was growing up, my neighborhood was about 95 percent African American. The schools I went to were mostly Jewish and my best friends were Asian, West Indian, African American, and Latino. The only Protestants I encountered were the members of my predominantly African American church. So while I saw a wide range of diversity growing up, it usually didn't include the white Protestant "norm." The only place I saw people like that was on television.

Coming from a community with a wide diversity of backgrounds and nationalities, I thought I was pretty good at relating to different kinds of people—until I moved to my first church. I was given the opportunity to serve an amazing congregation, but the catch was that I had to move from New York to the heart of the Midwest. When I went to visit the church, I found myself in a kind of "real America," which I never knew existed. I had to make a home in a community that I didn't understand, and I had to learn to navigate a culture that doesn't seem to know that it has a culture.

For example, the New York culture is very blunt and direct. You say what you mean and you mean what you say. But here, I've found that people rarely express a want or need directly, even if it's something as simple as saying "Call me back." Statements or questions that would seem ordinary or even passive in New York are heard as rude, aggressive, or even unpastoral here in the Midwest. Once, during my first Christmas at the church, I was told that we gave the children Christmas presents. That sounded great to me, so I went to the treasurer to get money to purchase the presents. She frowned and said, "I'm usually the one who gives the gifts to the children." I explained that it wasn't an intentional oversight and it was fine by me if she got the gifts, but she replied, "I don't need to do it." So I said, "But do you want to do it?" Thus began a five-minute-long, circular conversation. (Do you want to? I don't need to. Do you want to? I don't need to.) I finally realized that this native Midwesterner was never going to say, "I want to do it," and it was up to me to read what she was feeling, not only what she was saying.

As a new pastor, and a new member of this community, I am still learning how to translate implications into information and, more generally, to understand this culture and find a language, a connection and a home here in this real America. But I know that if I can do it here, then I will be living out my New York calling in this Midwest town and that it will help me be a more effective pastor. Therefore, in spite of the challenges, I am grateful for the experience and excited to serve this wonderful church.

8

Sisterhood or Sibling Rivalry?

Gender Balance and Working with Women

> *There is a special place in hell for women who do not help other women.*
>
> —MADELEINE K. ALBRIGHT

We often feel that women should be our allies. If anyone can understand the frustrations of scheduling, responsibility, and latent sexism, it is certainly another woman. Surely we are not the only ones who have to endure the trivial comments about our hair, our breasts, and our legs. Surely there are women in our congregations and denominations who "get it." We hope to find solace and understanding with our sisters in faith, and oftentimes we can.

While we can find relief in the common experiences of other women, we may also find that other women are our biggest challenge in our ministry. Whether we work alongside another female pastor or find ourselves facilitating the women's study or Vacation Bible School, we may face the frustrations of ministry from those women from whom we want the most support. Working within a community of other women can be a difficult task. It can be very deflating to reach out to women who we believe should understand, only to realize how very different our perspectives are. What happens when it's those women who cause the most stress?

The Great Debate

Who knew that scheduling a monthly committee meeting with eight women would come to define my first week as the new pastor? On the second day of my new job, I learned that my predecessor did not like to meet in person and preferred to do everything via mass e-mails to save time. At first I thought this was a bad idea and wanted to meet face-to-face. However, after the debacle that was scheduling, I totally understand the previous pastor's mass e-mail surrender.

The women's committee gathered at the church on a weeknight, bearing adorable homemade snacks to greet the new pastor. I had a lovely time getting to know this group of women—all of whom were mothers—and learned how long they had been church members and what brought them to this particular church. After we had mingled a bit, I asked them to get out their calendars so we could schedule a monthly meeting, face-to-face, that worked well for everyone. All eight women were enthusiastic about the idea of getting together instead of simply e-mailing, and I was practically giddy that my first big change at the church was going to be a wild success. We agreed that Tuesdays were the most soccer/hockey/basketball/ballet/

violin lesson–free evenings, so the second Tuesday of every month was the final answer.

Then came the Great Debate. The stay-at-home mothers wanted to meet over lunch; the mothers who worked outside the home wanted to meet for dinner. Period. There was no in between, no giving soul who thought that the morning or afternoon was even a possible, if unworkable, option. The group split in half with each team going after the other about whose schedules were more hectic and less flexible. After twenty minutes of what became a very heated discussion, one of them asked me what worked best for my schedule. Now, in any other social exchange this would be seen as polite. In this case, however, I felt like the vice president called in to cast the deciding vote in a congressional debate. My answer would do nothing less than fuel the fire, and I could feel sixteen eyes staring me down as I delivered the verdict.

So I gave my honest answer anyway, which was that 5:30 p.m. worked best for me with my existing Tuesday schedule, even though it was technically my time off. All the mothers who work outside the home said that was perfect for them, and the stay-at-home moms shrugged but agreed anyway. I thought we had found a good compromise for everyone, but as I was saying so, I was hit with a ton of bricks. One of the stay-at-home mothers said to me, "You just have no concept of the effect that missing dinner has on a family, what a sacrifice that is. You couldn't understand since you don't have kids."

Silence. The debate was momentarily at a standstill and I felt like waving the white flag of surrender, just forty-eight hours into my ministry. Finally another committee member chimed in, "Time away from her husband at dinner is also a sacrifice, so that's not really a fair comment." In my heart, I shouted, "Amen, lady!" but on the outside I just smiled weakly and asked them all to go ahead and write down their e-mail addresses. While I was grateful someone else responded so I didn't have to (they had only known me all of an hour after all!), I couldn't help wanting to give that committee member a piece of my mind. Everyone is asked to sacrifice something in service to God—is one dinner a month really such an unrealistic expectation? And husband or not, any time that's my personal time is a sacrifice. What would the defense be if I were single? Why do I need a defense? Why did these women need to justify every moment of their time, especially to each other?

Women can be our biggest challenge in ministry. Each woman faces her faith, family, and career in different ways. Even among women who may be of our same age, in our same career, or from a similar background, we can find unexpected headaches. Challenging ourselves to walk in another's clogs may not be enough; sometimes we simply find ourselves at odds with other women. As we've seen from the stories in other chapters, it might be the women in our churches who are most likely to criticize our shoes, ignore our attempts at establishing boundaries, or gossip behind our backs. One woman experienced this in the form of a gift in her mailbox:

> I had been away at a conference, so when I got back to the office I began sorting through mail and listening to messages. After putting about fifteen *Oriental Trading* catalogs in my recycling bin, I saw a small package. I opened it to find a bright floral makeup bag and a note from a female church member that read, "Your eyes look really puffy. Maybe these products will help you look less washed out." So there I sat with a pile of Vacation Bible School flyers, two invoices from Cokesbury, an invitation to a benefit concert, and free samples of antipuff eye cream, concealer, and cheek bronzer. Welcome back.

We also experience this backhanded passive-aggressiveness—and sometimes, full-on aggressiveness—among the women with whom we work. Much research has been done about the challenges of women in the workplace, particularly women working with other women. In *The New York Times* article "Backlash: Women Bullying Women at Work," Mickey Meece says,

> A good 40 percent of bullies are women. And at least the male bullies take an egalitarian approach, mowing down men and women pretty much in equal measure. The women appear to prefer their own kind, choosing other women as targets more than 70 percent of the time. In the name of Betty Friedan and Gloria Steinem, what is going on here?[1]

When we open ourselves to other women in the workplace, only to receive the cold shoulder, we can feel betrayed by the very people we hope will be our best colleagues.

Working with other female pastors can present its own set of challenges, particularly when we as young clergy women find ourselves working alongside an older female pastor. Their opinions, methods, and ways of thinking can seem frustrating, antiquated, or even antithetical to how we would approach our own ministry. While we know that they, our mothers in ministry, have probably endured many hardships in their own career, we can find ourselves frustrated by their approaches. This might manifest in different ways: Perhaps they seem too dogmatic or structured while we prefer a more laidback, organic, relationship-based approach to ministry. Or perhaps the opposite is true: We see them as too "maternal," falling into female stereotypes, while we aim for a professional, aggressive, career-minded ministry. However we find ourselves at odds with our female coworkers, it can be difficult to communicate our ideas and hear them out. It can feel like talking to our mothers—we love them, respect them, cherish the sacrifices they have made on our behalf, but we will inevitably disagree about certain subjects.

Yet if we can use our pastoral skills to put our biases aside and really hear them out, we can learn much from the women who have been in ministry for much longer than we. One woman states,

> I was in the first few weeks of my parish internship and was working alongside a pastor in her midfifties who had served the church for about a decade. She was beloved and highly respected, and I was both intimidated and thrilled at the thought of having her as a colleague and mentor. During my second week, she took me to lunch. I was expecting some insights into congregational care or at least a critique of my sermon. Instead she said, "I would like to ask you why you wear pants most days instead of skirts." I stared at her dumbfounded and stammered, "I don't know. I guess pants are just more comfortable." She pursed her lips and said, "Well, I have worn a skirt, and most days a suit, for the last twenty years, and I find it to be vital in the workplace. Most men wear dark suits. You have to dress the part if you want to be heard and taken seriously, and you won't be taken seriously in pants."
> At first I was angry and a little embarrassed that she didn't think I dressed the part, and I was not looking forward to buying a new wardrobe to blend in with the men in dark suits. And was this really the most pressing matter at hand, two weeks into my ministry? But she seemed serious, so I did a little experiment. I started wearing suits on the days we had staff or committee meetings with other men and learned she was exactly right. I was treated with more respect and was heard differently on the days I dressed up than on the days I didn't. It was an annoying lesson to learn—why are my ideas better when I'm wearing a skirt?—but I found myself being much less annoyed with her. She wasn't a stoic representative of an older generation, out to boss

me around. She was a survivor, and was graciously
giving me tips from her own experience.

In many ways, those mothers in ministry struggled so that
we could make decisions about our ministry. This plethora
of opportunities and decisions can complicate matters with
women our age. When it comes to work and family, women
seem to have more options than ever before, and every one of
us figures out our life priorities in different ways and at different
times. Like the woman in "The Great Debate," we might find
ourselves navigating between the women who choose to work
outside the home and the ones who choose to work within it.
We might look at the devoted mother, the aggressive career
woman, or the strong soul trying to be both and either empathize
with her or think that she is crazy. Working with women of a
similar background to us can encourage our ministries or drive
us crazy. When we have wrestled with the decisions of career,
marriage, faith, and family, we have to be open to the fact that
another woman, very similar to us, might have wrestled with
those exact same questions and come out with an entirely different list of priorities.

As uncomfortable as it is, we also have to remember that we,
too, can be a source of angst for the women with whom we work.
Ministry can be a trial by fire wherein we learn many, many lessons in just a few weeks or months. We might see that fresh-faced
intern or pastor, straight out of church camp, the living, breathing
definition of "green" and think, "Oh, no." Learning how to impart
our tenuous wisdom to others is an important endeavor. We must
embrace we will not always be the young ones in ministry and
that soon we may be asked to shepherd or mentor a young clergy
woman. How will we impart these experiences and lessons? How
will we listen to her hopes and plans and remember with clarity
how we felt not too long ago? Whether we work with women
who are younger, older, or of our own generation, finding ways
to embrace the diversity of our sisters in faith is arguably one of
the greatest challenges of our ministry.

Leaning on the Other

Perhaps not surprisingly, there are few stories in scripture that portray the dynamics of powerful women who work together. The great story of Ruth and Naomi, though, lends some insight into how this partnership is achieved. These two are thrown together when Naomi loses her husband and both of her sons and decides to return home to Judah. Orpah, the first daughter-in-law, decides to stay in Moab, but Ruth sticks with Naomi and speaks those inspiring words:

> Where you lodge, I will lodge; your people shall be my people, and your God my God. Where you die, I will die—there will I be buried. May the Lord do thus and so to me, and more as well, if even death parts me from you! (Ruth 1:16–18)

Despite Ruth's commitment, Naomi is still reeling from her losses and asks the people of Judah to call her "Mara," which means bitterness. It's only when Ruth finds her way into Boaz's lands that Naomi snaps out of it and helps Ruth to find a kind and wealthy husband that carries both of them out of poverty.

When we look at these women, we see two very different personalities. Ruth may be seen as a dedicated young woman who stands by her word, while Naomi is the tired, old mother-in-law. But the story tells us that both women were able to care for each other according to their strengths. When Naomi was devastated by loss, it was Ruth who shouldered the responsibility of caring for her by not abandoning her. But when Ruth was left wondering what to do with her life, it was Naomi who came to the rescue with a smart plan that gives the story its happy ending. Ruth is young and devoted but naïve and lacking in vision. Naomi is tired and deflated but also wise and experienced. Together, they represent a dynamic women's partnership in which they are able to challenge each other, care for each other, and lift each other's spirits—but they do so in very different ways, according to their gifts and their strengths.

As young women in ministry, we often appear enthusiastic and dedicated and yet lack practical knowledge about our ministries. And in return, our mothers in ministry can seem wise, but maybe, like Naomi, a little bitter. When we encounter other women in ministry, even those who frustrate us, we can look to Ruth and Naomi as a model of how we can inspire each other when we are lost, saddened, and lonely. We have to curb our desires to dismiss the words of our mothers, using our pastoral skills to listen in their critiques for the uncomfortable moments when they are judging us correctly.

Mary versus Martha

Whether we are working with colleagues or parishioners, we can find ourselves at odds with other women, which can drive our frustration and anger. One of the best stories in scripture presents this competition in the family feud known as Mary versus Martha:

> Now as they went on their way, he entered a certain village, where a woman named Martha welcomed him into her home. She had a sister named Mary, who sat at the Lord's feet and listened to what he was saying. But Martha was distracted by her many tasks; so she came to him and asked, "Lord, do you not care that my sister has left me to do all the work by myself? Tell her then to help me."
>
> But the Lord answered her, "Martha, Martha, you are worried and distracted by many things; there is need of only one thing. Mary has chosen the better part, which will not be taken away from her." (Lk. 10:38–42)

Many a devotion and Bible study has been written about Mary and Martha. The debate usually centers on which woman respected or loved Jesus more. It seems that Luke is indeed trying to make a point about which sister is engaging in life-giving ministry and which one is just busy. Even Jesus seems to take a side. But as Jane Carol Redmont says,

This story is not one of those cases where taking sides will be life-giving. Why pit the sisters against each other, or their ministries of domestic management and service on the one hand and attention to the living Word on the other?[2]

When we are forced to take one side or the other in this argument, we can quickly end up like the women in "The Great Debate," yelling at each other about whose priorities are better and whose schedule is harder, resigning to passive communication rather than life-giving relationship.

We have all had times when we feel more like one woman than the other and can empathize with the competitive nature of living with and among the women—whether we are related by blood or not. We can emulate Mary, genuinely intent on hearing God's Word; we can also often be Martha, struggling to get everything done and looking for help from other women that doesn't always materialize. We can even look at Jesus' words and think, "You may be right, but your words are not particularly *helpful* in this situation." To his credit, Jesus is asked to step in and offer a verdict in this sibling squabble, and his point may be that without Mary's attention to the Word, Martha's energies will eventually fail. Yet we also realize that Martha's actions are life-giving as well: sustaining our bodies with feast and food that gives us energy, while Mary's dedication offers sustenance for our souls. Both are necessary, and the ministries of both Mary and Martha are needed in God's creation.

If we are honest, it is often easier to critique other women than deal with what is actually going on within ourselves. This is especially true when we are exhausted and stressed. Many times we too are upset about many things when only one thing is needed. We get caught up in our own funks and lose sight of the main thing we are called to do in ministry. Yet time and time again Jesus goes against all social norms and, with great love and compassion, allows us to sit at the feet of grace. When we take the side of one sister, choosing the path of either Mary or Martha, and label ourselves as either one or the other, we are indeed cheating our families, our congregations, and ourselves. Our intent should not be to compare Mary and Martha, to judge them, or to judge ourselves based on which sister we feel most resembles us. Instead, we should endeavor to find ways to serve God in both diligent study and task completion. As church leaders, we are to share the undeserved grace with all we meet, recognizing that we are all some aspect of Mary and Martha, and appreciate each woman's unique way of showing respect, love, and hospitality to the Son of God.

She Drives Me Crazy

As young women in ministry, we are called to have an open heart to the wisdom of women, both young and old. We have the unique privilege of learning from women who are true pioneers in a field that is still, in almost all cases, dominated by men. In our churches, we work alongside talented, dedicated women who sacrifice their time and energies to the church, shaping and growing our ministries as we serve and are served by them. No doubt some of our most infuriating situations will be caused directly by the women we work with, but the joy of being modern women is that we all have more options and opportunities. Figuring out how to navigate all these opportunities is part of our freedom and our responsibility.

> She. Drove. Me. Crazy. That is all there is to say about her. She absolutely, always, without fail, made my life completely miserable.
>
> I had been in my first call for a few years when they hired her to serve as our senior minister. I was so excited to have a strong, intelligent, caring woman at our church—a woman with the reputation for being an exceptional person in pretty much every way. How much would I be able to learn from her? What could she teach me about living the ministerial life? Where could our ministry make the

biggest difference, and how could we grow our church and community together?

That was the first week. By the second week, I knew that something was off. She was never there. She came in late, she left early, and she wouldn't call me back. I was the one teaching every class, making sure the Sunday school teachers were happy, and planning for worship. I took all the calls, presided over all the funerals, met with all the new parents, and made sure that sidewalks were swept. I was furious; our former minister had been a wonderful leader, loved by the whole congregation, but the new pastor was just . . . vacant. I was neglecting my family, putting on weight, and felt run down and tired all the time. And because I was trying to maintain some dignity, I didn't feel like I could speak with anyone about what was going on. "Suffering in silence" took on a whole new meaning, and I found myself stuck between a congregation I dearly loved and a boss that I wanted to strangle.

And then the unthinkable happened—a young, beautiful, dedicated mother in the church was diagnosed with extremely aggressive cancer, and she died in just a couple of months. Everyone was shocked and saddened. As soon as I got the call that she had died, I felt completely guilty. I hadn't really realized how bad the cancer was and didn't even get a chance to really say good-bye. What if I had had some time in the last few months that I could have spent with her? If I wasn't covering all the responsibilities at every moment of every day, maybe I would have had some time to notice how this young mother was suffering. How could I be a minister to a family I had let down?

After I got the call, I tried to call the senior minister's cell phone, but of course it went to voice mail. So I gathered what courage I had and went over to their house. When I walked into the living room, I was shocked to see that she was already there. She was holding their newborn, gently rocking the baby and praying with the grieving husband. Their little daughter, just barely three years old, was sitting on the couch, leaning against her, sucking her thumb with sleepy, teary eyes. I could barely breathe. In such a moment, when I felt lost and useless, she was an anchor. She was calm and caring and comfortable. I literally sat at her feet and watched her minister with such tenderness and love that I felt God's presence even in this tragedy. We stayed for an hour or so and then left together.

When we got to our cars, she turned to me and said, "For the last few months, I have been meeting with her most days of the week. Of course, there wasn't much we could do, but each day that we could, I would take her to the beach. She felt some comfort there, and we would talk or sit in silence, whatever she wanted." I stood there, speechless. She continued, "I didn't share this with you or the congregation because she wanted to keep her illness private. But I could do all of this because you were taking care of everything else. So thank you."

I realized then how much I had already learned from her, even though she drove me crazy. I realized that ministry wasn't only about how much time we spent at the church and how many programs we had or students we taught. I *was* able to keep everything running, while she was able to spend time with a scared, dying woman. At that moment, I realized that despite my anger, ministry was happening—in my life, in her life, in this family's life, and in the life of our congregation. It didn't really matter how we got there; it only mattered that we had arrived, together.

She still drives me crazy sometimes. I wish she was around more often, but I know that together, we are ministering to people when they most need it. And I am proud to learn from her.

9

Struggling for Sabbath

Time Management and Finding Balance

> *No cure that fails to engage our spirit can make us well.*
>
> —VICTOR FRANKL

Much has been written about the pastor's schedule and how it can wreak havoc on our personal lives. When everyone else is gearing up for work on a Monday morning, we are trying to wind down from a long Sunday. When everyone else has the weekend off, we are most certainly on. When the holidays roll around, we roll up our sleeves and get to work. We put in a full day's work at the office, and then after the workday is done, our real work begins. Our vacations are punctuated by worries that someone may end up in the hospital, and we will have to unexpectedly return to deal with grief and crisis. We rarely have two days off in a row, and we might even live next door, attached to, or in the same building as our work.

Almost no pastor works forty hours a week. We usually work much longer and harder than we expect or can handle, giving the best of ourselves to our congregations and ministries while hoping that our personal lives will work themselves out. Sometimes they do. But increasingly, pastors of both genders find themselves stressed and burned out. *The New York Times*, drawing on the research of the Clergy Health Initiative, put it clearly:

> The findings have surfaced with ominous regularity over the last few years, and with little notice: Members of the clergy now suffer from obesity, hypertension, and depression at rates higher than most Americans. In the last decade, their use of antidepressants has risen, while their life expectancy has fallen. Many would change jobs if they could.[1]

But as a leading research institute said, this news seems to be surprising to everyone . . . except clergy.[2] We are perhaps too aware of the stress and strain that our congregations and denominations place on us—and how much stress we bring on ourselves. Many young clergy women come to ministry with plans, excitement, and energy, but we can quickly fall into the patterns that have plagued many of our colleagues. When we do that, we can find ourselves exhausted and burned out faster than we ever imagined.

People Talk

People talk. I mean—people talk. That's what I learned (among other things) in my first year of ordained ministry. People would talk if I didn't come in to work at 8:00 in the morning. They would talk if I didn't stay until 5:00. They would talk if I couldn't make the evening meeting. They would talk if I wasn't sitting at my desk when the phone rang, and they would talk if it seemed I wasn't out in the community enough. In or out, up or down, working or not, it didn't matter—people talked.

I really did try, in that first year, to set some clear limits for others and myself. I was the first female pastor this small congregation had ever had, and I wanted too much to be successful in their eyes. But I also knew I had responsibilities to myself. I planned for a day of Sabbath, but for some reason I could never make it happen. I read all about clergy burnout and told myself that my ministry was a marathon and not a sprint, but I still found myself working too hard and too long. So I tried to work smarter—I got organized, developed a schedule, relied on my parishioners, and visited with colleagues. But nothing seemed to help. At the end of each and every day, I was tired, cranky, and always far, far behind. And people talked about that, too.

And really, I don't blame them. As a solo pastor in this little church, I knew I was the main person they were looking for. If I wasn't available when they needed me, or I couldn't drop everything to be with them in that moment, they felt abandoned and frustrated—and they talked to whoever would listen about their frustrations. But I don't blame myself either. With several evening meetings weekly, and an average of at least three other meetings, with a husband who works evenings, with a home to clean and laundry to do and meals to make, with a daughter to raise and a family to build, I simply could not make the pieces of the puzzle come together. I realized that I had a choice to make. Either I could meet expectations or I could stay married, stay sane, and let people talk. I choose the latter.

All pastors, no matter their gender, can get caught up in working. Without close attention to ourselves, our schedules can become our lives, our congregations can become more important than our families, and our daily responsibilities can become more immediate than our spiritual health. When we encounter the needs of a church, we can quickly become overwhelmed and convinced that the longer and harder we work, the more we can fix in this broken world. We often feel we should be available, and *want* to be available, at any and all times to respond to our congregation.

We are entrusted to be there when our congregants experience great joys and sorrows: when the babies are born, when the mother dies, when the youth gets accepted to the college of his dreams. We want to be faithful in our sermon writing and study while not passing up the opportunity for coffee with the young adult who just lost her job. If we are on the way to yoga and receive a phone call that someone was in an accident, we turn around and go directly to the hospital. And while this isn't wrong, and most of us would regret *not* going, when do we make up that personal time? How do we find any sense of routine amid the unplanned adventures and roller coasters in the lives of our flock? And how do we continue to keep our sense of self while living into our callings as daughters, sisters, friends, wives, mothers, and now pastors?

Many pastors suggest that we must find time for "self-care," but even our attempts at self-care can be frustrating if we only rely on ourselves. When we are stressed for time, having a massage, taking a trip, and even praying a daily devotional can feel like one more thing added on to a list of chores that we will never accomplish. Self-care is an important commitment, reminding us that we, ourselves, are also a part of the body of Christ. But as pastors we cannot only rely on ourselves for our own spiritual nourishment. We have to find appropriate ways to let others share that burden and opportunity, even as we give openly and thoroughly to others. As one pastor named Lillian Daniel says, "It seems odd that as Christians, we would tell one another that the answer to such woes lies in ourselves, and in our own will power and our own resolutions to do better."[3] We have to truly identify what activities, people, and places can provide care for us, without relying on clichés, unrealistic expectations, and inappropriate relationships.

What can be even more frustrating is that many members of our congregation work very hard, as well. When we lament the three-hour evening meeting, it's important to remember that the dedicated parishioner also put in a full day's work at their office and then booked it over to the church for a long meeting. Many people in many different professions live life on call—at any given time they might be called in to work, just like we are. Few people can take a long vacation away from their jobs, and even when they do, they are distracted by e-mails and phone calls, just like we are. And many people work in emotionally stressful jobs, even more difficult and distressing than ours. A recent seminary graduate told it like this:

> In seminary they told us over and over again that ministry was *so hard*. If you even think that you can be happy doing something else, they said, then do it, because the only way you will survive in ministry is if it is the only way you can envision yourself being happy. I'm too new to know if that's true, but sometimes I look at my responsibilities and put them against some of my friends and parishioners. It feels so self-indulgent to even suggest that our work is *that much harder* than the work of other people. I guess in fifty years, I'll know who was right.

For young women in these different professions, the pressures of work can seem even more immediate. If we feel the need to "prove ourselves," we may take the extra steps to get to work early and leave late. If you don't have children, it's easy to stay the extra hours or volunteer to cover the meeting so someone with a family can get home. When we do have families, we might feel guilty for being apart from them, while simultaneously feeling guilty for missing opportunities at work. On the occasions when we do attempt to set some boundaries, and acknowledge that we are working too long, too much, or too often, we might feel the pressure from others to put in the same kinds of hours they do, even when we know it's unhealthy. A young pastor recalled,

> My first church had a very clear work ethic. It was a large congregation and your work was based on a simple equation: the longer you worked, the better you were. If you were not available to do something, you could be sure that another staff member would come along and do the job, proving that they were more dedicated than you, a better pastor than you, and maybe even a better Christian. Daily, thoughtless, perpetual sacrifice was the name of the game. It was like something out of a Wall Street movie, a black-and-white work ethic that I incorrectly believed was relegated to other professions. And sadly, I played the game just as hard and as well as the others.

Even if we maintain a normal number of work hours, the realities of church life can still cause us frustration. The upheaval of the weekend schedule can be particularly hard for young clergy. Many of us have grown accustomed to enjoying Friday or Saturday nights out with friends and family, and the single pastor might hope for the occasional date night in the midst of frantic sermon writing. Saturday evenings can be particularly distressing when we remember the fun other people are having while we are trying to get to sleep early. When the rest of the community is relaxing and blowing off some steam, we are preparing for the biggest day of the week. One woman told this story:

> There was a terrible snowstorm on Saturday night, and the entire city was covered in two feet of snow. On Sunday morning, I was watching the news, trying to figure out how on earth I was going to get to church. The news anchor made this brilliant observation: "Well,

at least it's Sunday and no one has to go to work." I screamed at the TV, "Some of us do!"

The pressure of being constantly available and constantly working can make us forget what is work and what is not. Our parishioners become our friends, and our social outlets can be work events, but when it's difficult to carve out time off, we tend to take whatever social avenues we can get. For example, here is a weekly rundown from a young clergy woman:

- Mondays: two devotional groups in the morning, one Bible study at lunch, one Bible study in the afternoon, and a long committee meeting at night
- Tuesdays: early worship, staff meetings, planning for Sunday worship, and then congregational leadership meetings at night
- Wednesdays: children's playgroup in the morning, standing lunch with the city pastors' group, dinner, classes, and youth group at night
- Thursdays: hospitals, hospitals, hospitals, and then usually dinner with a parishioner
- Fridays: a day off, but really a day for sermon writing, rehearsal dinners, and funerals
- Saturday: pretty quiet, unless there is a 5K, service project, mission trip, lock-in, carnival, fundraiser, retreat, art show, choir rehearsal, class, wedding, or funeral—and then only if the sermon is done
- Sundays: fine-tuning the sermon, teaching Bible study, worship, coffee hour, more worship, more coffee hour, brunch with young adults, meeting with women's group, youth group, and mission meeting that night

At first glance we might say, "These all sound like fun activities!" and in a way, many of them are. But take another look: There is almost no room here for anything unrelated to the church. Without some very intentional scheduling, it is almost impossible to maintain balance between our work and the rest of our lives. Again, many people in many different professions feel like this, and in some ways we are but one example of the work epidemic that plagues our modern culture. But the challenge is that, as pastors, we are called to demonstrate a more excellent way. We cannot let ourselves buy into the idea that work will set us free. Our freedom comes from knowing and serving God, yet ironically, we let ourselves be consumed by our work *in the name of* serving our God, a God who constantly reminds all of us to, "Be still, and know that I am God!" (Ps. 46:10).

Rethinking the Example

If the Sabbath is meant as a day of rest and worship, Jesus definitely did not take the day off. There are several examples in scripture of Jesus healing, eating, and teaching on the Sabbath. Luke tells one story like this:

> On one occasion when Jesus was going to the house of a leader of the Pharisees to eat a meal on the Sabbath, they were watching him closely. Just then, in front of him, there was a man who had dropsy. And Jesus asked the lawyers and Pharisees, "Is it lawful to cure people on the Sabbath, or not?" But they were silent. So Jesus took him and healed him, and sent him away. Then he said to them, "If one of you has a child or an ox that has fallen into a well, will you not immediately pull it out on a Sabbath day?" And they could not reply to this. (Lk. 14:1–6)

Looking at this story in light of our work schedules can seem overwhelming. Jesus seems to be making the point that every day is an opportunity for ministry. Anything righteous, helpful, or necessary that you might do on Saturday should be done on Sunday as well. And in this respect, Jesus is definitely right. If you ran across a lost child, an injured friend, or anyone in desperate need of help, wouldn't you stop and help—even if it's your day off? Jesus' point to the Pharisees is that we cannot follow the letter of the law when it works directly against the spirit of the law. We must be willing to sacrifice our need for Sabbath in the face of those in true need. And yet as pastors, it can seem like there is always someone in need, no matter the day or time. So to follow Jesus' example would mean that we are always available, no matter if it's our Sabbath or not.

Jesus may set this example, but when faced with the unending work hours of ministry, it can be helpful to remember something very basic: We are not Jesus. Rather than thinking of ourselves as the one who always needs to be available on the Sabbath, we need to remember that in the work of ministry, we are more similar to that lost child, injured friend, or dispirited parishioner. We are not called to healing in our communities at anytime, and every time. Rather, we are called to service in Christ, as human, fallible, and yes, tired people who need healing just as much as those we are called to give it to. As one scholar says, when Jesus heals on the Sabbath, he "is not offering a model for seven day a week ministry . . . There is no 'Go and do likewise,' at the end of the story, no 'You have heard it said . . . but I say to you' here or elsewhere with respect to Sabbath law."[4] Jesus sets himself against the hypocrisy of the Pharisees who would use something as precious as the Sabbath to score a cheap point. But he does not suggest that we abandon the Sabbath because there is always important work to be done. Instead, he asks us to reconsider what it means to keep the Sabbath.

Keeping Sabbath

When it comes to the Sabbath, there is no lack of opinions in scripture. Every book in the Pentateuch and every gospel mentions the importance of remembering the Sabbath and keeping it holy. We can ignore these clear instructions. But given our proclivity to abandon the Sabbath, perhaps a more helpful scripture text comes from the gospel of John:

> I am the true vine, and my Father is the gardener. He cuts off every branch in me that bears no fruit, while

every branch that does bear fruit he prunes so that it will be even more fruitful. You are already clean because of the word I have spoken to you. Remain in me, and I will remain in you. No branch can bear fruit by itself; it must remain in the vine. Neither can you bear fruit unless you remain in me . . . You did not choose me, but I chose you and appointed you to go and bear fruit—fruit that will last. (Jn. 15:1–4, 16)

Just as we see Jesus healing and teaching on the Sabbath, we also hear Jesus saying, "No branch can bear fruit by itself." If we think we can heal all the wounds of our congregations, wipe all the tears, and celebrate every joy by being available every moment, then we are most certainly wrong. And if we think we can be the "all-things pastor" to every sheep in our flock because we do indeed love them, again we hear Jesus' words: "Neither can you bear fruit unless you remain in me." Unless we remain rooted in Christ's love and God's claim on our lives, we cannot fully live into our calling as clergy women. Jesus acknowledges that we did not *choose* this calling. Instead, we have been appointed by God to go out into the world to bear fruit.

As we take this command seriously, our need for Sabbath is even more obvious. We serve a God who desires a relationship with us and promises over and over again that we are not, and never will be, alone. We are not alone in this life and we are not alone as young clergy women. We are called to remain in the love of God, not only in the times we feel we are inadequate or tired, but at all times. We find rest, refreshment, and restoration when we take the time to be nurtured by our family and friends both inside and outside the church.

The fruits of our labors are not measured by the number of hours we spend in the office or how much time we spend away from our families. Rather, we young clergy women bear fruitful service when we leap joyfully into this complicated world of ministry that God has created, honoring ourselves, showing mercy to others, and above all, giving our lives over to the God who created us to be the leaders that we are and aim to be. This is how we bless our own hearts and bless the hearts of others, for unless we remain in the one true vine, we can bear no fruit at all.

Choices

As pastors, we have to acknowledge that our schedules, our commitments, and our very lives are going to be different from other professions. We need to take time and opportunities for relaxation and Sabbath when we can and do our best to model a responsible work ethic for our congregation, even when they want us available at any moment. Recognizing this, God calls us to make choices and sacrifices—both to ourselves and to our churches—and to create a working environment that takes into account the seriousness of our callings and the seriousness of our calling for Sabbath:

Technically, in my denomination, we are supposed to work thirty-five hours per week. While completely unfunny, that is a joke.

Although ordained in the United States, I was given the opportunity to work at a large church in Europe. I quickly realized this opportunity was too good to miss and so I accepted the position. Working at a church in Europe was very different from an American style of ministry. In my church, they operate within a parish ministry where those who are located in your area technically are your parishioners. Beyond the hundreds that were on the church rolls, there were thousands of others who relied on the services of the church and the presence of a minister. Mine was the only church in this large city for the denomination, so I was the pastor for just about everything.

With all that, my first year of full-time ministry was stressful but going well. After a year at the church, I learned that the other minister at the church had taken a position elsewhere and I would be left, for a time, on my own. My responsibilities increased greatly, and I was stretched to the limits. But I loved the church, I loved the city, and I loved this awesome and challenging opportunity.

Things have been difficult, but I made some specific choices that have made this ministry work. I learned to delegate more and involve church leaders in new and helpful ways. I purchased a car to help with the increase of hospital and home visits. I hired someone to clean and organize my house, giving me a few more precious hours a week. I became even more diligent about taking a full day off a week, and I am intentional about filling that time with things that give me pleasure. Rather than collapsing on the couch, I try to garden, cook, and enjoy my friends. My congregation does their best to honor my limited, but essential, time off.

I am aware of the sacrifices I have made for this ministry. I know that I may not be able to do this job forever and that the long hours and stress of being the only pastor for such a large number of people is not for everyone. But, for me, I love this church, and I feel blessed to be a part of the lives of the members of the congregation. It has been quite the challenge, but I am glad that God has given me the strength and wisdom to enjoy this ministry.

Epilogue

Stories are the heart of scripture and the means by which we tell the truth of the saving life, death, and resurrection of Jesus Christ. Similarly, we aimed for the stories to be the heart of *Bless Her Heart*. We hope that the tales in this text have inspired and empowered you to tell a little, or a lot, of your own story. If you would like to join in the conversation, we invite you to respond to *Bless Her Heart* at www.blessherheartstories.org and to journey with the Young Clergy Women's Project at *Fidelia's Sisters*, www.youngclergywomen.org.

To that end, we'd like to offer one final story, not from a young clergy woman, but a young clergyman. He says,

> Above my desk in my pastor's study is a picture of my graduating class from seminary. Of the 21 M.Div. graduates, 14 are women and dear friends of mine. Throughout our three-year journey together, we've often talked about the complications of women in ministry, and now as several of them are ordained, most of them are serving small, rural churches. They often share with me their stories and I hear their words reflected in this book.

The face and place of ministry is changing, and we have great hope for our future—both for clergy women and clergy men. We are stronger when all of us in ministry share our stories. When we speak with care and honesty, all clergy—male and female, young, old, and somewhere in between—can

119

learn from each other's experiences. Another young clergy woman shared,

> Women—and men—that have shared this journey with me have supported and shaped my view of myself in ministry in positive ways. It's in the stories that we share that I've found peace and hope for the ways God is moving in our world.

Whoever you are and however you got here, we hope you have laughed, cried, been moved, been challenged, seen things differently, and had moments of "thank goodness I'm not the only one" throughout your reading. We greatly enjoyed working on this together and had many laughs and tears throughout the process of collecting stories from amazing young clergy women. We continue to be humbled and honored by all who trusted us and encouraged us to write this and are blessed to call them our sisters in faith.

May God continue to bless you and keep you, and may your hearts always be blessed.

Peace to you all,
Ashley-Anne and Stacy

Notes

Preface

[1]"Emily," *What Not to Wear*, TLC, Discovery Communications, February 5, 2010.

Acknowledgments

[1]Montreat Conference Center website, http://www.montreat.org/about/mission-statement.

Introduction

[1]"Clergywomen's Experiences in Ministry: Realities and Challenges," Advocacy Committee for Women's Concerns, a ministry of the General Assembly Council, Presbyterian Church (USA), 2005, 9, http://oga.pcusa.org/publications/clergywomenexp03.pdf.

[2]See research from the Duke Clergy Health Initiative, http://www.divinity.duke.edu/initiatives-centers/clergy-health-initiative. The Duke Clergy Health Initiative, a $12 million, seven-year program intended to improve the health and well-being of the 1,600 United Methodist elders and local pastors serving churches in North Carolina, has found, among many other things, that "the rates of disease for clergy were much higher for diagnoses of diabetes, arthritis, asthma, and high blood pressure" and "pastors reported that their rate of depression is roughly double that of all people in the United States." Recent studies completed by CREDO Institute (http://www.episcopalcredo.org) and the Sustaining Pastoral Excellence program of the Lilly Endowment (http://www.faithandleadership.com/programs/spe) have published similar findings.

[3]Andrew J. Weaver, Kevin J. Flannelly, David B. Larson, Carolyn L. Stepleton, and Harold G. Koenig, "Mental Health Issues Among Clergy and Other Religious Professionals: A Review of Research," *Journal of Pastoral Care & Counseling* 56, no. 4 (2002), accessed February 19, 2011, http://healthcarechaplaincy.org/userimages/Mental%20Health%20Issues%20Among%20Clergy%20and%20others.pdf.

⁴Mark A. Chaves, *National Congregations Study, 1998 and 2006* (Ann Arbor, MI: Inter-university Consortium for Political and Social Research, 17 November 2009).

Chapter 1: Pedicures for the Pastor

¹"Guide My Feet," African-American Spiritual, *Presbyterian Hymnal (Pew Edition): Hymns, Psalms and Spiritual Songs* (Louisville: Westminster/John Knox Press, 1992).

Chapter 2: I Know You Are, but What Am I?

¹Robert Wuthnow, *After the Baby Boomers: How Twenty- and Thirty-Somethings Are Shaping the Future of American Religion* (Princeton, NJ: Princeton University Press, 2007), 9.

²Joan Chittister, "The Story of Ruth: Moments of Loss and Faith," *The Chicago Sunday Evening Club* 14 (2001), accessed 6 February 2010, http://www.csec.org/csec/sermon/Chittister_4415.htm.

Chapter 3: Romancing the Reverend

¹See further discussion in David Carr's *The Erotic Word: Sexuality, Spirituality and the Bible* (New York: Oxford University Press, 2003).

Chapter 4: Hemlines and Homiletics

¹Anne Lamott, *Plan B: Further Thoughts on Faith* (New York: Riverhead, 2005), 202.

Chapter 6: Jesus Wept

¹Henri Nouwen, "Forgiveness: The Name of Love in a Wounded World," *Weavings* 7, no. 2 (March/April 1992), 15.

²See Henri Nouwen's *The Wounded Healer: Ministry in Contemporary Society* (New York: Random House, 1979).

Chapter 7: Make Yourself at Home

¹Sam Martin, "Singing the Lord's Song in a Strange Land," *Day1*, 20 August 2006, accessed 13 March 2011, http://day1.org/1004-singing_the_lords_song_in_a_strange_land.

²Eric Barreto, "Commentary on First Reading, Acts 16:9–15," Luther Seminary's *Working Preacher*, 9 May 2010, accessed 14 March 2011, http://www.workingpreacher.org/preaching.aspx?lect_date=5/9/2010.

Chapter 8: Sisterhood or Sibling Rivalry

¹Mickey Meece, "Backlash: Women Bullying Women at Work," *The New York Times*, 9 May 2009, accessed 6 February 2010, http://www.nytimes.com/2009/05/10/business/10women.html.

[2]Jane Carol Redmont, "The Mary-Martha Double Bind: Lectionary Reflections for Pentecost 7C," *A Globe of Witnesses*, 18 July 2004, accessed 29 October 2009, http://www.thewitness.org/agw/redmont071504.html.

Chapter 9: Struggling for Sabbath

[1]Paul Vitello, "Taking a Break from the Lord's Work," *The New York Times*, 1 August 2010, accessed 4 March 2011, http://www.nytimes.com/2010/08/02/nyregion/02burnout.html.

[2]Wayne Whitson Floyd, "Clergy Burnout," the Alban Institute, accessed 3 March 2011, http://www.alban.org/conversation.aspx?id=9169.

[3]Lillian Daniel, "What Clergy Do Not Need," Weblog entry, the Call and Response blog on Faith and Leadership, an offering of Leadership Education at Duke Divinity School, 12 February 2009, accessed 4 March 2011, http://faithand leadership.com/blog/02-12-2009/lillian-daniel-what-clergy-do-not-need.

[4]Mary Hinkle Shore, "Jesus and the Peaceable Kingdom," *Pilgrim Preaching*, 5 December 2004, accessed 22 November 2009, http://maryhinkle.typepad.com/pilgrim_preaching/isaiah.